KT-156-008

EVERYDAY POSITIVE THINKING

THE POSITIVE THOUGHTS IN THIS BOOK HAVE BEEN EXCERPTED FROM THE FOLLOWING HAY HOUSE CARD DECKS*:

Abraham-Hicks Well-Being Cards, by Jerry and Esther Hicks: **www.abraham-hicks.com**

Attitude Is Everything™ Cards, by Keith D. Harrell: **www.keithharrell.com**

Comfort Cards, by Max Lucado: **www.maxlucado.com**

Dream Cards, by Leon Nacson: **leon@hayhouse.com.au**

Empowerment Cards, by Tavis Smiley: **www.tavistalks.com**

The Four Agreements Cards and *The Mastery of Love Cards,* by DON Miguel Ruiz: **www.miguelruiz.com**

Healing Cards, by Caroline Myss: **www.myss.com,** and Peter Occhiogrosso: **www.joyofsects.com**

Healing the Mind and Spirit Cards, by Brian L. Weiss, M.D.: **www.brianweiss.com**

Healthy Body Cards, I Can Do It® Cards, Power Thought Cards, and *Wisdom Cards,* by Louise L. Hay: **www.hayhouse.com**

Heart and Soul, by Sylvia Browne: **www.sylvia.org**

Tips for Daily Living Cards and *Until Today Cards,*
by Iyanla Vanzant: **www.innervisionsworldwide.com**
Women's Bodies, Women's Wisdom Healing Cards,
by Christiane Northrup, M.D.: **www.drnorthrup.com**
Words of Wisdom for Women Who Do Too Much,
by Anne Wilson Schaef: **www.livinginprocess.com**
Zen Cards, by Daniel Levin: **www.hayhouse.com**

*Some excerpts have been adapted for clarity and tense.

All of the above are available at your
local bookstore, or may be ordered by visiting:

Hay House USA: **www.hayhouse.com**
Hay House Australia: **www.hayhouse.com.au**
Hay House UK: **www.hayhouse.co.uk**
Hay House South Africa: **orders@psdprom.co.za**
Hay House India: **www.hayhouseindia.co.in**

If Life Is a Game, These Are the Rules Cards,
by Chérie Carter-Scott, Ph.D.: **www.drcherie.com**
Inner Peace Cards and *The Power of Intention Cards,*
by Dr. Wayne W. Dyer: **www.drwaynedyer.com**
Kryon Cards, by Lee Carroll: **www.kryon.com**
Magical Mermaids and Dolphins Oracle Cards,
by Doreen Virtue, Ph.D.: **www.angeltherapy.com**
Manifesting Good Luck Cards (Growth and Enlightenment), (Love and Relationships), (Success and Money),
by Deepak Chopra, M.D.: **www.chopra.com**
MarsVenus Cards, by John Gray: **www.marsvenus.com**
Miracle Cards, by Marianne Williamson:
www.marianne.com
Money Cards, by Suze Orman: **www.suzeorman.com**
Organizing from the Inside Out Cards,
by Julie Morgenstern: **www.juliemorgenstern.com**
The Prayer of Jabez™ and *Secrets of the Vine™ Cards,*
by Dr. Bruce Wilkinson: **www.brucewilkinson.com**
Self-Care Cards, by Cheryl Richardson:
www.cherylrichardson.com
The 7 Habits of Highly Effective People® Cards,
by Stephen R. Covey: **www.franklincovey.com**

EVERYDAY POSITIVE THINKING

LOUISE L. HAY
AND FRIENDS

HAY HOUSE, INC.
Carlsbad, California
London • Sydney • Johannesburg
Vancouver • Hong Kong • Mumbai

Copyright © 2004 by Hay House, Inc.

Published and distributed in the United States by: Hay House, Inc.: www.hayhouse.com • ***Published and distributed in Australia by:*** Hay House Australia Pty. Ltd.: www.hayhouse.com.au • ***Published and distributed in the United Kingdom by:*** Hay House UK, Ltd.: www.hayhouse.co.uk • ***Published and distributed in the Republic of South Africa by:*** Hay House SA (Pty), Ltd.: orders@psdprom.co.za • ***Distributed in Canada by:*** Raincoast: www.raincoast.com • ***Published in India by:*** Hay House Publications (India) Pvt. Ltd.: www.hayhouseindia.co.in • ***Distributed in India by:*** Media Star: booksdivision@mediastar.co.in

Editorial supervision: Jill Kramer • *Design:* Amy Rose Szalkiewicz

All rights reserved. No part of this book may be reproduced by any mechanical, photographic, or electronic process, or in the form of a phonographic recording; nor may it be stored in a retrieval system, transmitted, or otherwise be copied for public or private use—other than for "fair use" as brief quotations embodied in articles and reviews without prior written permission of the publisher. The intent of the contributors is only to offer information of a general nature to help you in your quest for emotional and spiritual well-being. In the event you use any of the information in this book for yourself, which is your constitutional right, the contributors and the publisher assume no responsibility for your actions.

Library of Congress Control Number: 2003106479

ISBN 13: 978-1-4019-0295-7
ISBN 10: 1-4019-0295-2

09 08 07 06 10 9 8 7
1st printing, February 2004
7th printing, February 2006

Printed in Canada

A Few Words from Louise L. Hay

We at Hay House are so blessed to have a wonderful family of very special authors. We want to share this selection of thoughts from our positive affirmation cards (listed in the front) to support you with your daily thoughts. All is well! Life is good!

Louise L. Hay

The thoughts you choose to think and believe right now are creating your future. These thoughts form your experiences tomorrow, next week, and next year.

– Louise L. Hay

Release the need to blame anyone, including yourself. We're all doing the best we can with the understanding, knowledge, and awareness we have.

– Louise L. Hay

Send out love
and harmony,
put your mind and body
in a peaceful place,
and then allow the
universe to work in
the perfect way that
it knows how.

– Dr. Wayne W. Dyer

Intention is a force in the universe, and everything and everyone is connected to this invisible force.

– Dr. Wayne W. Dyer

Joy is a pure state of bliss, and it's attained by bringing comfort and relief to other people. Doing so will bring joy to your life every day.

– Sylvia Browne

Milton said that within everyone, there is heaven and there is hell. Choose heaven—release the regret and the guilt. Remember that through love, God will ease your pain and cement you back together.

– Sylvia Browne

To be successful in your chosen career or work endeavor, you must release any present karmic conditioning that declares, "I can't do this." You can!

– Deepak Chopra, M.D.

When you recognize that you're a human being who sometimes makes mistakes, you won't get caught up in the illusion of self-importance.

– Deepak Chopra, M.D.

The things that matter most in this world are those that carry no price tag, for they can neither be bought nor sold at any price.

– Suze Orman

True generosity lies not in how much money you *have*, but whether the money you have coming in and going out passes through your heart back out into the world.

– Suze Orman

When life presents more challenges than you can handle, delegate to God. He not only *has* the answer, He *is* the answer.

– Tavis Smiley

We're all here for a purpose. Meditate on your mission, then use your gifts and talents to live your life on purpose. In doing so, you'll become an unending magnet for miracles.

– Tavis Smiley

In asking for miracles, we're seeking a practical goal: a return to inner peace. We're not asking for something *outside* us to change, but for something *inside* us to change.

– Marianne Williamson

Life is like a book
that never ends.
Chapters close,
but not the book itself.
The end of one physical
incarnation is like the
end of a chapter, on
some level setting up
the beginning of another.

– Marianne Williamson

Highly proactive people don't blame circumstances, conditions, or conditioning for their behavior. Their behavior is a product of their own conscious choice.

– Stephen R. Covey

An abundance mentality flows out of a deep inner sense of personal worth and security. It stems from the paradigm that there's plenty out there . . . and enough to spare for everybody. It opens possibilities, options, alternatives, and creativity.

– Stephen R. Covey

Look for things to feel good about, and watch how everything in your life will unfold to reflect that good-feeling vibration.

– Abraham-Hicks

Your decision to reach for a thought that feels good is a powerful decision, for it serves you in many ways. The better-feeling thought reverberates within you, opening passageways to well-being that reach far beyond this one good-feeling thought.

– Abraham-Hicks

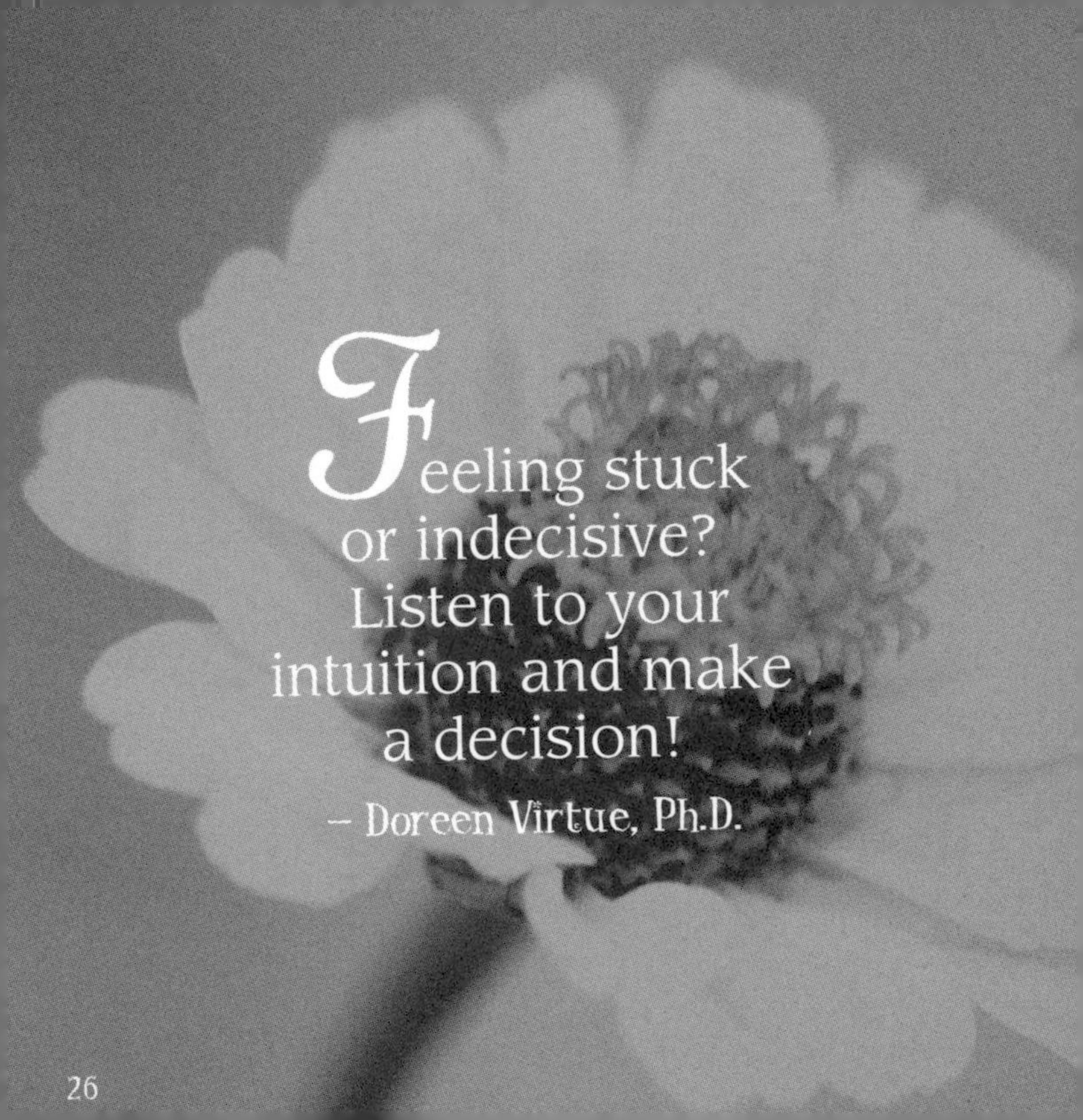

Feeling stuck or indecisive? Listen to your intuition and make a decision!

– Doreen Virtue, Ph.D.

Surround yourself with positive people and situations, and avoid negativity.

– Doreen Virtue, Ph.D.

Say only what you mean. Avoid using the word to speak against yourself or to gossip about others. Use the power of your word in the direction of truth and love.

— DON Miguel Ruiz

The whole world can love you, but that love will not make you happy. What *will* make you happy is to share all the love you have inside you. That is the love that will make a difference.

— DON Miguel Ruiz

It's easy to get lost in endless speculation. So today, release the need to know why things happen as they do. Instead, ask for the insight to recognize what you're meant to learn.

– Caroline Myss
and Peter Occhiogrosso

Mercy is a rare word, one hardly spoken. What are merciful actions? Not judging another; speaking with kind words; thinking compassionate thoughts about others. May acts of mercy come your way.

– Caroline Myss
and Peter Occhiogrosso

Know your thoughts and assumptions, and realize that you may have swallowed them whole. Learn from your experiences. Discard outdated beliefs and thoughts.

– Brian L. Weiss, M.D.

Wisdom is achieved slowly and is the active expression of knowledge in your everyday life. Loving service is the highest wisdom.

– Brian L. Weiss, M.D.

Release your perfectionism. The process of life is always changing. Demanding perfection holds the universe in a straitjacket.

– Christiane Northrup, M.D.

a true partnership provides a safe place to take risks. It also encourages mutual growth and evolution.

– Christiane Northrup, M.D.

The key to happiness is realizing that it's not what *happens* to you that matters, it's how you choose to respond.

– Keith D. Harrell

You don't have to let what others say affect you negatively. Others may say the words, but *you* choose your attitude.

– Keith D. Harrell

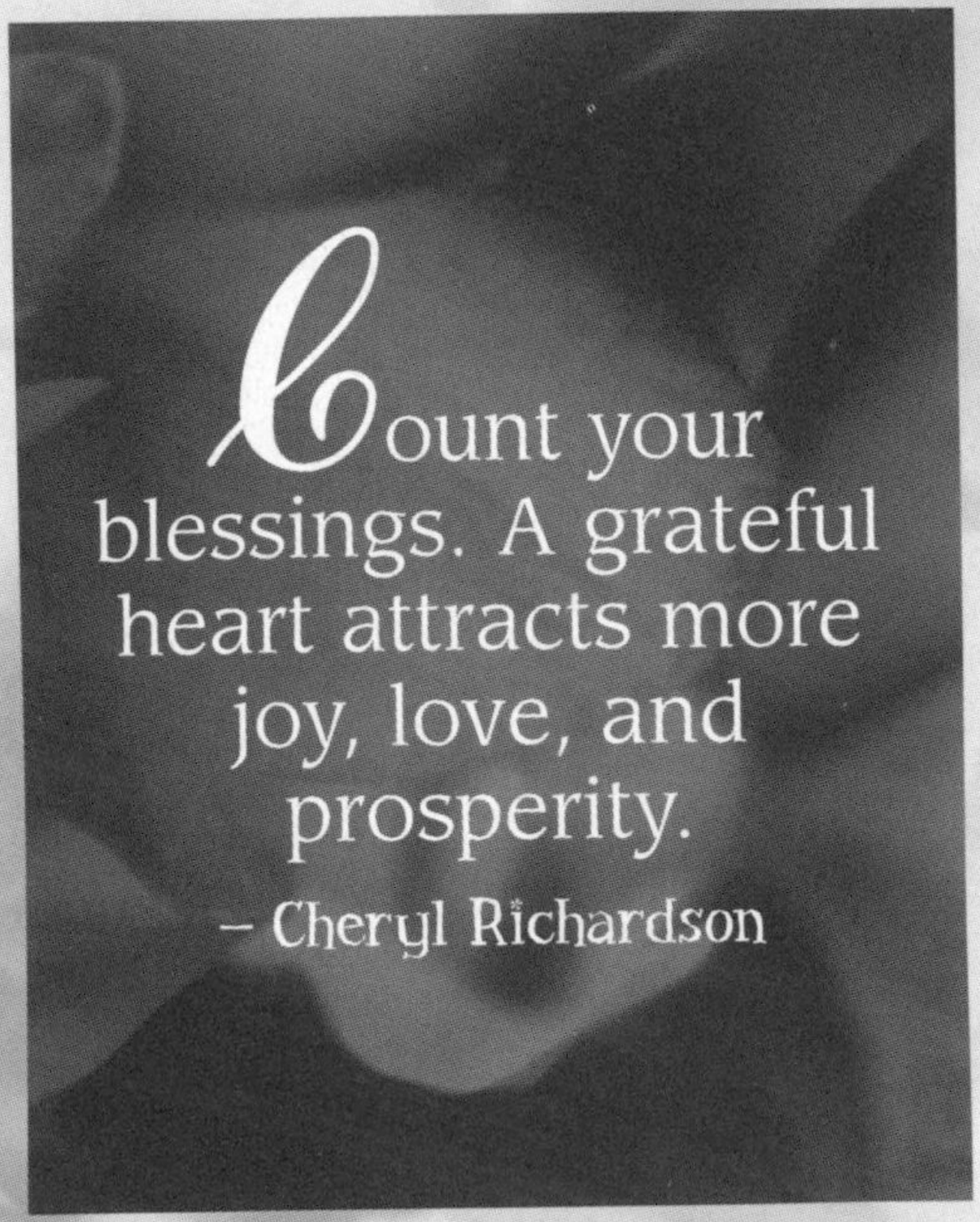
Count your blessings. A grateful heart attracts more joy, love, and prosperity.
– Cheryl Richardson

Tell the truth. Integrity is the key to living an authentic life.

– Cheryl Richardson

Tests of faith
are various trials
and hardships that
invite you to surrender
something of great
value to God
even when you have
every right not to.

– Dr. Bruce Wilkinson

It doesn't matter whether you're short of money, people, energy, or time. What God invites you to do will always be greater than the resources you start with.

– Dr. Bruce Wilkinson

Until today, you may have realized that it's not loving to remain in situations that aren't working for you, hoping they'll get better. *Just for today,* realize that when you've done all you can do, there's simply no more you can do, and it's not healthy or productive to try!

– Iyanla Vanzant

Haven't you had enough change in your life? Relationships change. Health changes. The weather changes. But the God who ruled the earth last night is the same God who rules it today.

– Max Lucado

Devote yourself to something or someone and honor that choice— no matter what.

– Chérie Carter-Scott, Ph.D.

Find the inner strength required when confronting danger, difficulty, or opposition.

– Chérie Carter-Scott, Ph.D.

These are your times, bought and paid for with thousands of years of incarnations and work by your selves. Claim this time! You are empowered to do so. This is why you are dearly loved.

– Kryon

God
is love, and love
is the most
powerful force
in the Universe.
It will protect
and serve you.

– Kryon

Sometimes you just need a good scream. Remember, a good "scream-a-logue" directed at no one is often more effective than a dialogue or monologue.

– Anne Wilson Schaef

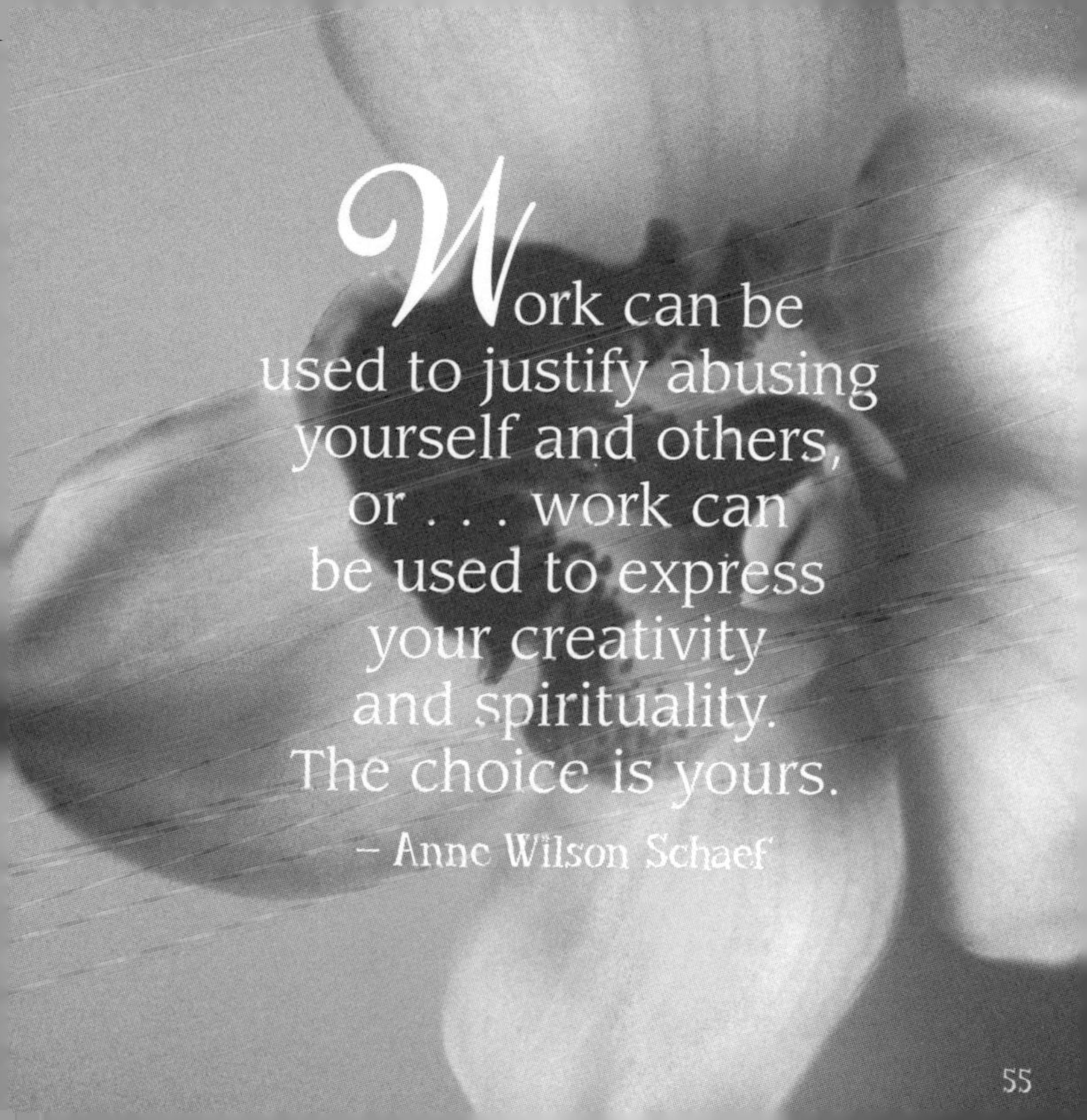

Work can be used to justify abusing yourself and others, or . . . work can be used to express your creativity and spirituality. The choice is yours.

– Anne Wilson Schaef

Always know when you've pushed beyond your limits, and then bring yourself back to balance.

– Leon Nacson

Be genuinely concerned for the welfare and growth of others. Feel their strengths.

– Leon Nacson

Each day, accept everything that comes to you as a gift. At night, mentally give it all back. In this way, you become free. No one can ever take anything from you, for nothing is yours.

– Daniel Levin

Feel the pain of others. Understand their struggles and disappointments, their hardships and inadequacies, and open your heart to them. Realize that everyone is doing the best they possibly can. Judge no one. But rather, cradle all of humanity in your heart.

– Daniel Levin

When you make the effort to pay attention to the sights, sounds, smells, and sensations around you, you're encouraging yourself to live in the present moment.

– Deepak Chopra, M.D.

Be confident enough to be able to voice your opinions without fear of recrimination. As such, you will inspire the same action in others.

– Deepak Chopra, M.D.

When you're feeling fear with respect to money, repeat to yourself: "I am strong, I am strong, I am strength itself." You will find that your anxiety will be replaced by a new feeling of confidence.

– Suze Orman

When it comes to your money, do what makes you feel safe, sound, and comfortable. Trust yourself more than you trust others. Believe it or not, you and you alone have the best judgment when it comes to your money.

– Suze Orman

Regardless of your race, religion, or political affiliation, never hesitate to question those in authority.

– Tavis Smiley

Avoid the enticement to be mean or argue. Allow others to be right. As far as you're concerned, be peaceful with everyone you encounter.

– Tavis Smiley

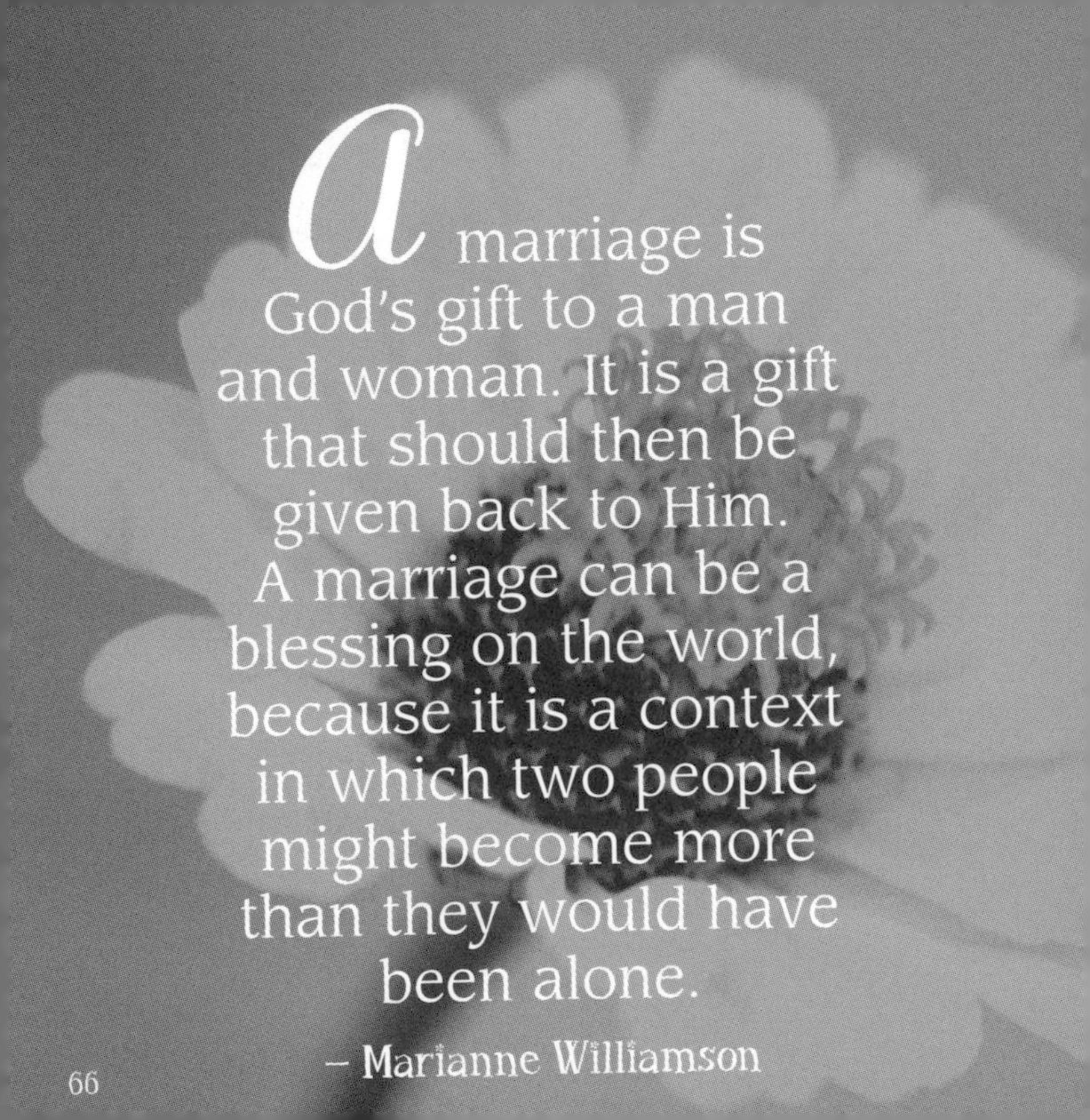

A marriage is God's gift to a man and woman. It is a gift that should then be given back to Him. A marriage can be a blessing on the world, because it is a context in which two people might become more than they would have been alone.

– Marianne Williamson

Personal growth can be painful, because it can make us feel ashamed and humiliated to face our own darkness. But our spiritual goal is the journey out of fear-based, painful mental habit patterns, to those of love and peace.

– Marianne Williamson

Don't take insults personally, sidestep negative energy, and look for the good in others. You can utilize that good—as different as it may be—to improve your point of view and enlarge your perspective.

– Stephen R. Covey

Create affirmations with these basic ingredients: They're *personal, positive,* in the *present tense, visual,* and *emotional.* Then, each day, visualize the realization of these affirmations. You'll find that your behavior and circumstances will change for the better.

– Stephen R. Covey

Trying to limit anybody about anything defies the Laws of the Universe. It cannot be done. You cannot control others, but you can control—and create—your own reality.

– Abraham-Hicks

You could have every disease known to man within you today, and if you chose different-feeling thoughts tomorrow, they would all leave your body. The key is to not give any unwanted thing much attention. When it doesn't feel good, turn your attention someplace else.

– Abraham-Hicks

Try different ventures and experiences as a way to grow and learn.

– Doreen Virtue, Ph.D.

You're more powerful than you realize. It's safe for you to be powerful!

– Doreen Virtue, Ph.D.

Whatever people do, feel, think, or say, don't take it personally. Others are going to have their own opinion according to their belief system, so whatever they think about you is not about *you*, but it is about *them*.

– DON Miguel Ruiz

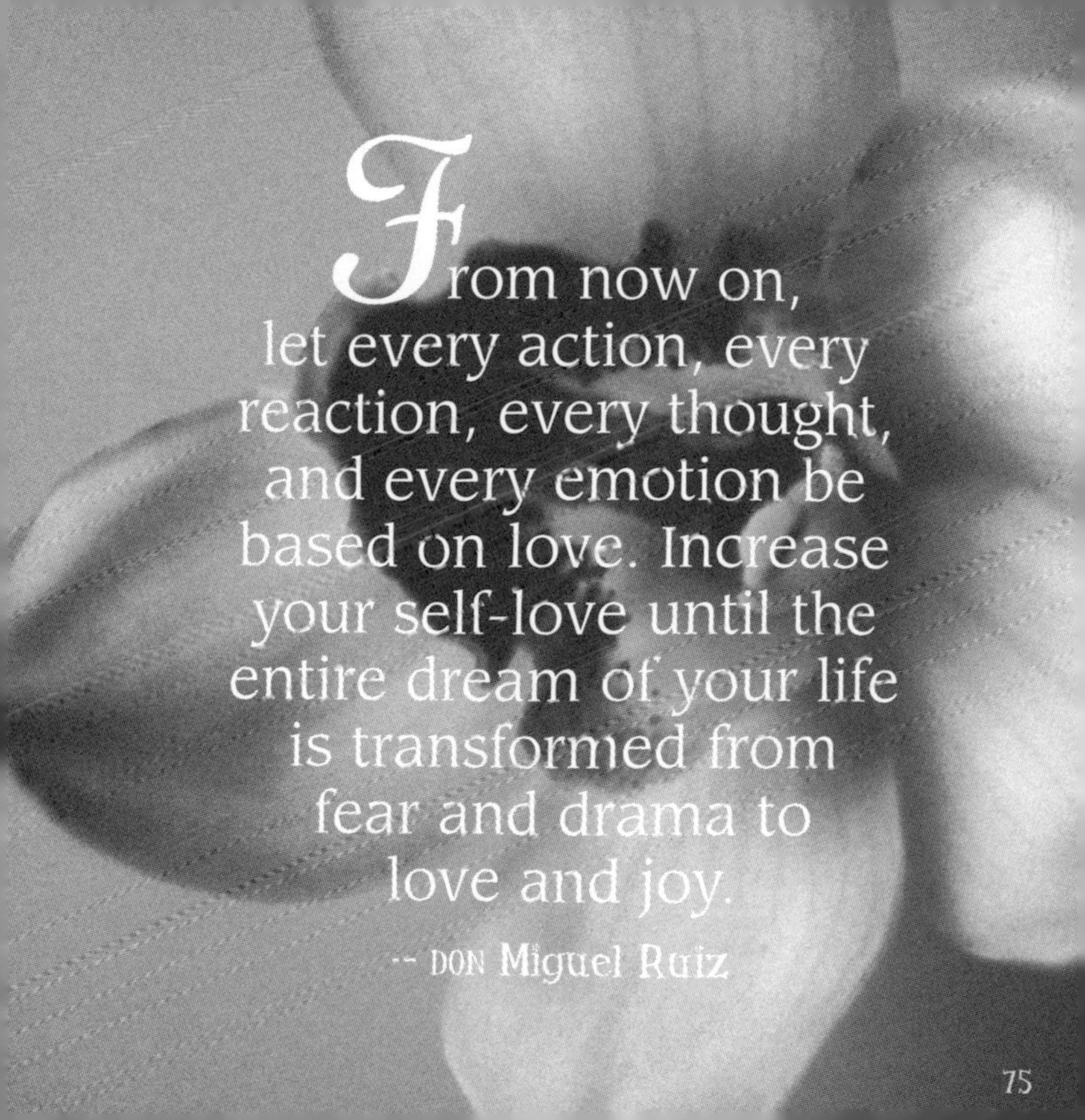

From now on, let every action, every reaction, every thought, and every emotion be based on love. Increase your self-love until the entire dream of your life is transformed from fear and drama to love and joy.

-- DON Miguel Ruiz

Healing requires that you admit the truth about yourself. Is there someone you hate or something you crave? Are you an addict? Recognizing your struggles is the first step toward healing.

– Caroline Myss
and Peter Occhiogrosso

Consider this amazing possibility: You incarnated on this earth just to experience the joy of being alive. Do you even know what gives you joy? Do something about that today.

– Caroline Myss
and Peter Occhiogrosso

You're not merely your physical self. You existed before you came into your physical body, and you will exist after you leave your body.

– Brian L. Weiss, M.D.

People are constantly changing and growing. Don't cling to a limited, disconnected, negative image of a person in the past. See that person now.

– Brian L. Weiss, M.D.

Acknowledge the consequences of failing to express who and what you really are. True self-expression is based on self-examination, integrity, honesty, and a willingness to change.

– Christiane Northrup, M.D.

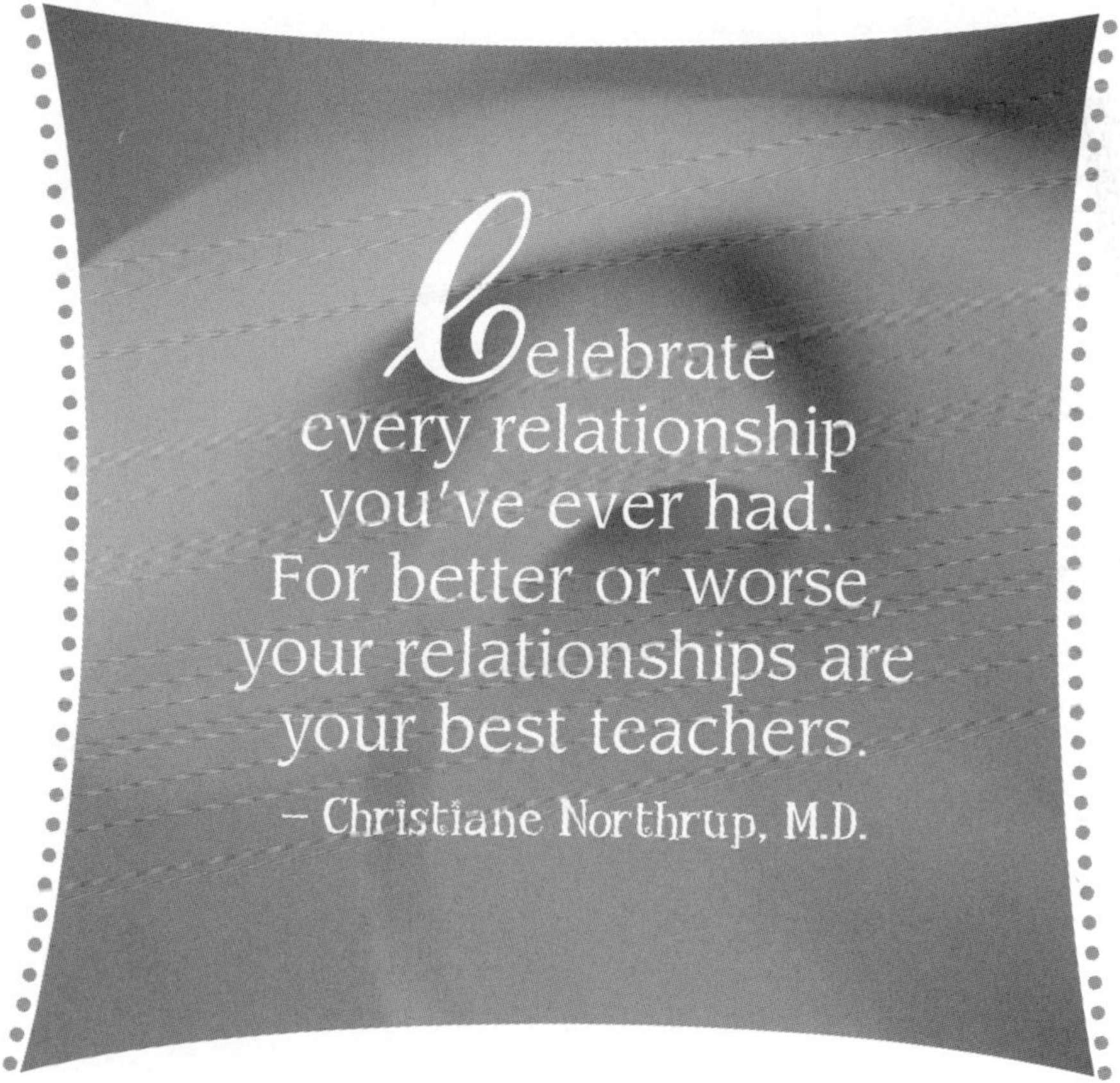
Celebrate
every relationship
you've ever had.
For better or worse,
your relationships are
your best teachers.
– Christiane Northrup, M.D.

Attitude is the foundation and support for everything you do. It's the key element in the process of controlling your destiny.

– Keith D. Harrell

For true happiness, look within yourself. It's difficult to be happy if you rely on outside resources.

– Keith D. Harrell

Let go
of the need
to control.
Trust in the
wisdom
of a divine plan.
– Cheryl Richardson

Honor your top priorities. If it's not an absolute *yes*, then it's a *no*.

-- Cheryl Richardson

God wants to hear your requests, your worries, and your praise and thanks. Risk being honest, and expect His insight in return.

– Dr. Bruce Wilkinson

Asking is the beginning of receiving. Through a simple believing prayer, you can change your future. You can change what happens one minute from now.

– Dr. Bruce Wilkinson

Until today, you may have been holding on to secret thoughts and feelings. You may have been afraid to open yourself up to self-examination or outside scrutiny. Just for today, be willing to release those things stored in your heart and mind that are causing you discomfort.

– Iyanla Vanzant

What would it take for you to forget all your troubles? Are you *willing* to simply forget all your troubles today? When you remove your attention from a problem, it gets bored and moves away!

– Iyanla Vanzant

A man scores points with a woman if he does his best to contribute. A woman scores points with a man if she lets him off the hook when he makes a mistake.

– John Gray

When a woman becomes overwhelmed, she retreats to her "well" to recharge. When a man becomes angry, he needs to go to his "cave" to cool off.

-- John Gray

Circulate dormant possessions. Don't hang on to items you aren't using just because you spent good money on them, because if you ever need them again, they'll probably find their way back to you.

– Julie Morgenstern

Remove the obstacles. Untangle the clutter that's standing between you and the productive, fulfilling life that you crave.

– Julie Morgenstern

God sleeps through storms and calms the winds with a word. Cancer does not trouble Him, and cemeteries do not disturb Him. He was here before they came. He'll be here after they're gone.

– Max Lucado

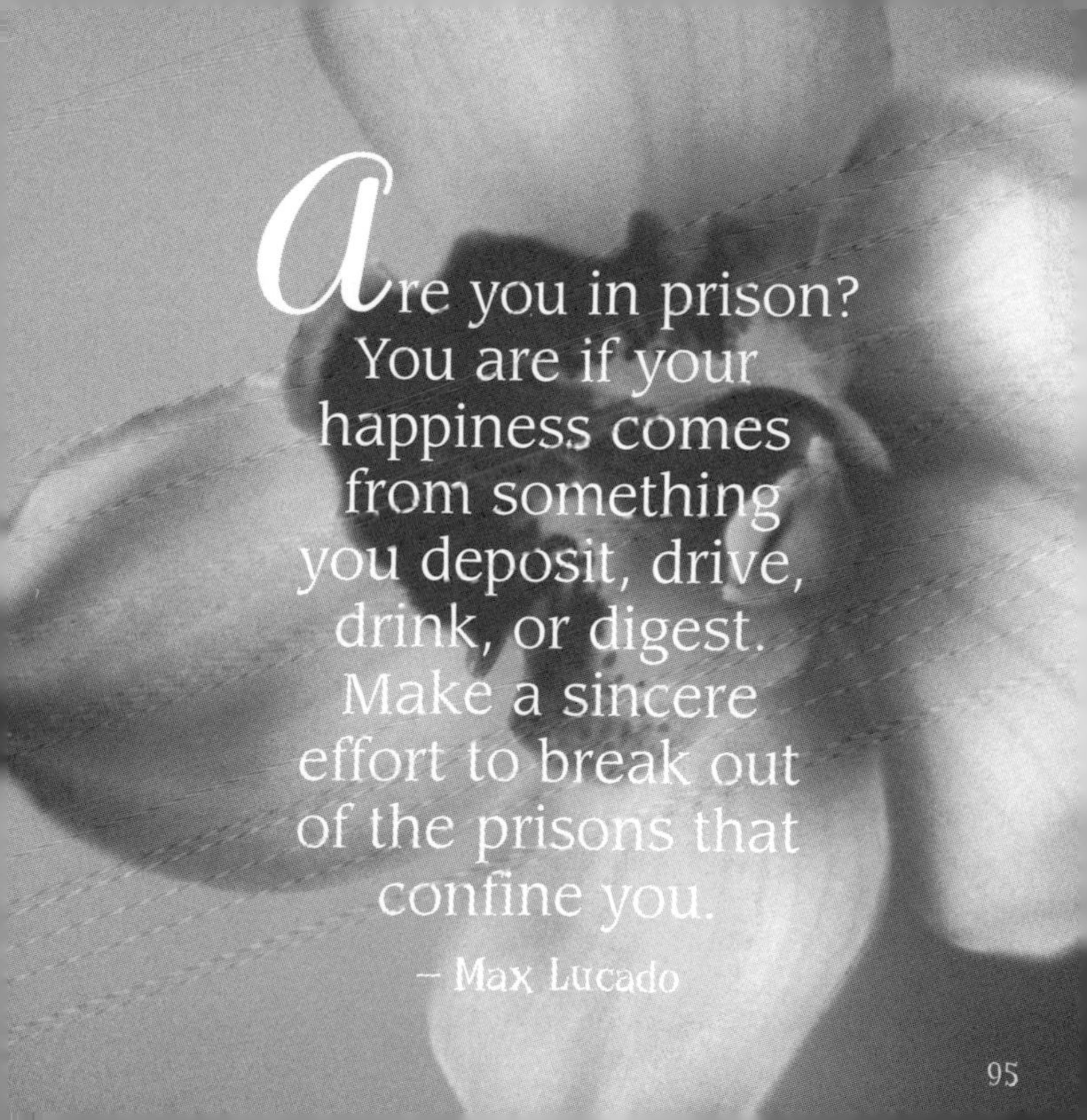

Are you in prison? You are if your happiness comes from something you deposit, drive, drink, or digest. Make a sincere effort to break out of the prisons that confine you.

– Max Lucado

Be confident and modest about your own merits, and understand your limitations.

– Chérie Carter-Scott, Ph.D.

Acknowledge that you are the source of your manifestations.

– Chérie Carter-Scott, Ph.D.

Feeling stuck on your path? Celebrate it! Celebrate the knowledge that all is relative and that you may be stopped so that others may catch up. Would you deny them the participation in what you've created?

– Kryon

There's nothing that existed in your past that cannot be changed *now*. You are the creator of the past and the future. Therefore, you create the whole *now*, even the things that you feel are unchangeable.

– Kryon

Have compassion for your parents' childhoods. Know that you chose them because they were perfect for what you had to learn. Forgive them and set them free.

– Louise L. Hay

Know that you are the perfect age. Each year is special and precious, for you shall only live it once. Be comfortable with growing older.

– Louise L. Hay

The intention of this universe is manifested in zillions of ways in the physical world, and every part of you, including your soul, your thoughts, your emotions, and your physical body are a part of this intent.

– Dr. Wayne W. Dyer

Act as if anything you desire is already here. Believe that all that you seek you've already received, that it exists in spirit, and know you shall have your desires filled.

– Dr. Wayne W. Dyer

People may try to ruin your reputation, and this can hurt. But remember, it can only hurt your *feelings*. The world will forget, so don't hold on to bad publicity or what others say. You and God know the truth, so let the rest of it go.

– Sylvia Browne

If you don't move your body, your brain thinks you're dead. Movement of the body will not only clear out the "sludge," but will also give you more energy. Treat your body like a car--keep it tuned up and it will run for a very long time.

– Sylvia Browne

The greatest secret to making money and being successful is helping *other* people make money and be successful.

– Deepak Chopra, M.D.

The small things you do every day—smiling at a stranger or paying someone a compliment—bring you closer to your spiritual truth, the purity of your soul.

– Deepak Chopra, M.D.

Financial freedom comes when you take care of the people and the places around you, and you offer your services to God.

– Suze Orman

Money enables you to make choices, and the choices you make with your money ultimately add up to your values. It follows, too, that how much money you have will mirror how much you *value* your money.

– Suze Orman

Loosen up.
You are never too old,
too professional,
or too accomplished
to laugh and be silly.
Allow yourself to play.
Let your inner child out
and enjoy your life.

– Tavis Smiley

Be open, honest, and honorable in all your endeavors. Establish high standards, principles, and values for yourself, then kick it up a level. In everything you do, be true to *you*.

– Tavis Smiley

Look into the faces of the people you see in public each day, and silently say: "The light of God in me salutes the light of God in you." Do it for five minutes minimum. I defy you to do this each day and *not* be happy.

– Marianne Williamson

Intimacy means that we're safe enough to reveal the truth about ourselves in all its creative chaos. If a space is created in which two people are totally free to reveal their walls, then those walls, in time, will come down.

– Marianne Williamson

Your example flows naturally out of your character, the kind of person you truly are. Your character is constantly radiating and communicating. From it, others come to instinctively trust or distrust you and your actions.

– Stephen R. Covey

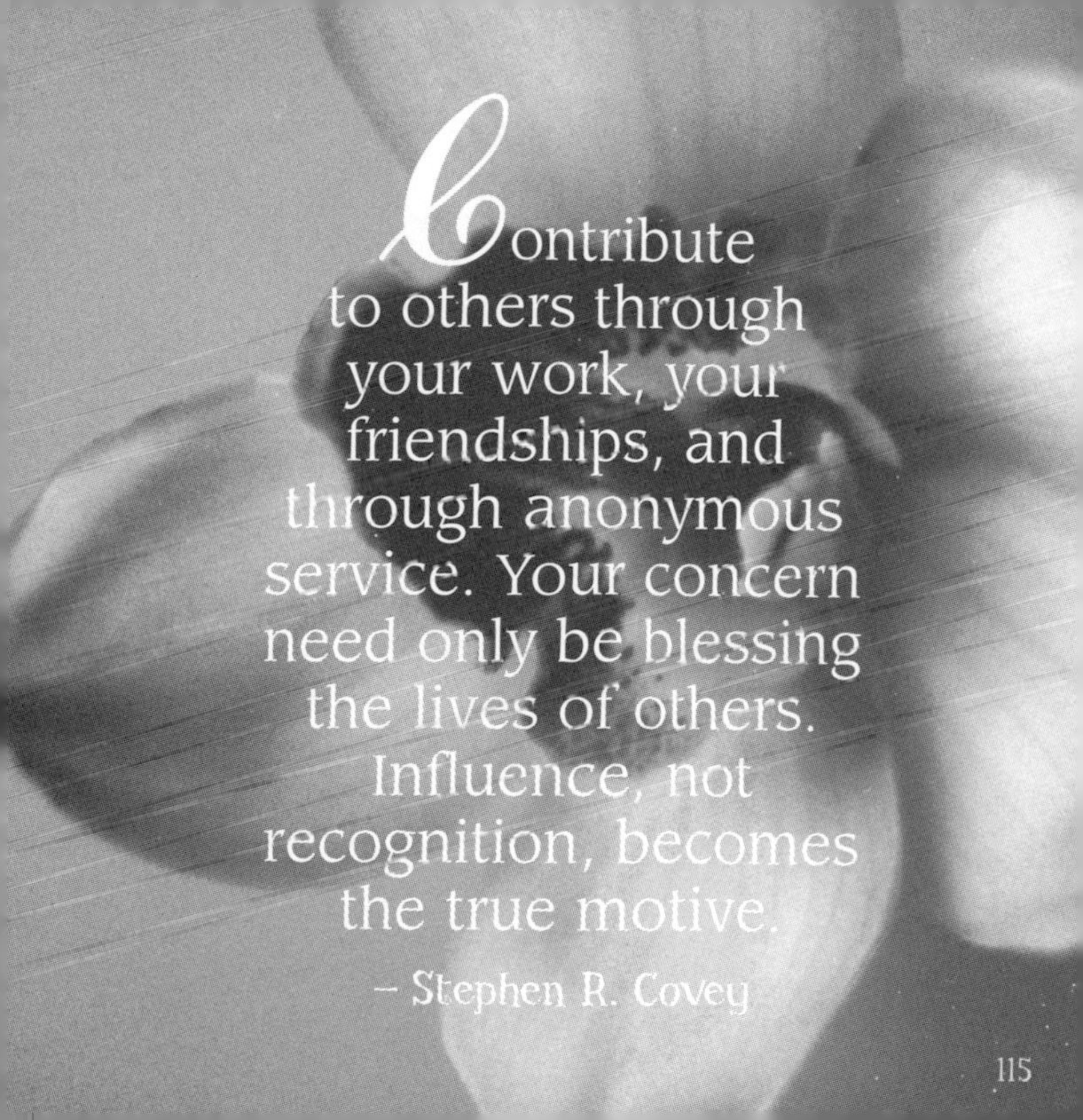

Contribute to others through your work, your friendships, and through anonymous service. Your concern need only be blessing the lives of others. Influence, not recognition, becomes the true motive.

– Stephen R. Covey

No one can create in your experience, for no one can control where you direct your thoughts. On the path to your happiness, you will discover all you want to be, do, or have.

– Abraham-Hicks

Even though you will return home at the end of any vacation, the idea of your holiday is not to complete it as quickly as possible so that you can check it off of your list. The idea of your vacation—and of this life—is to have a joyous experience.

– Abraham-Hicks

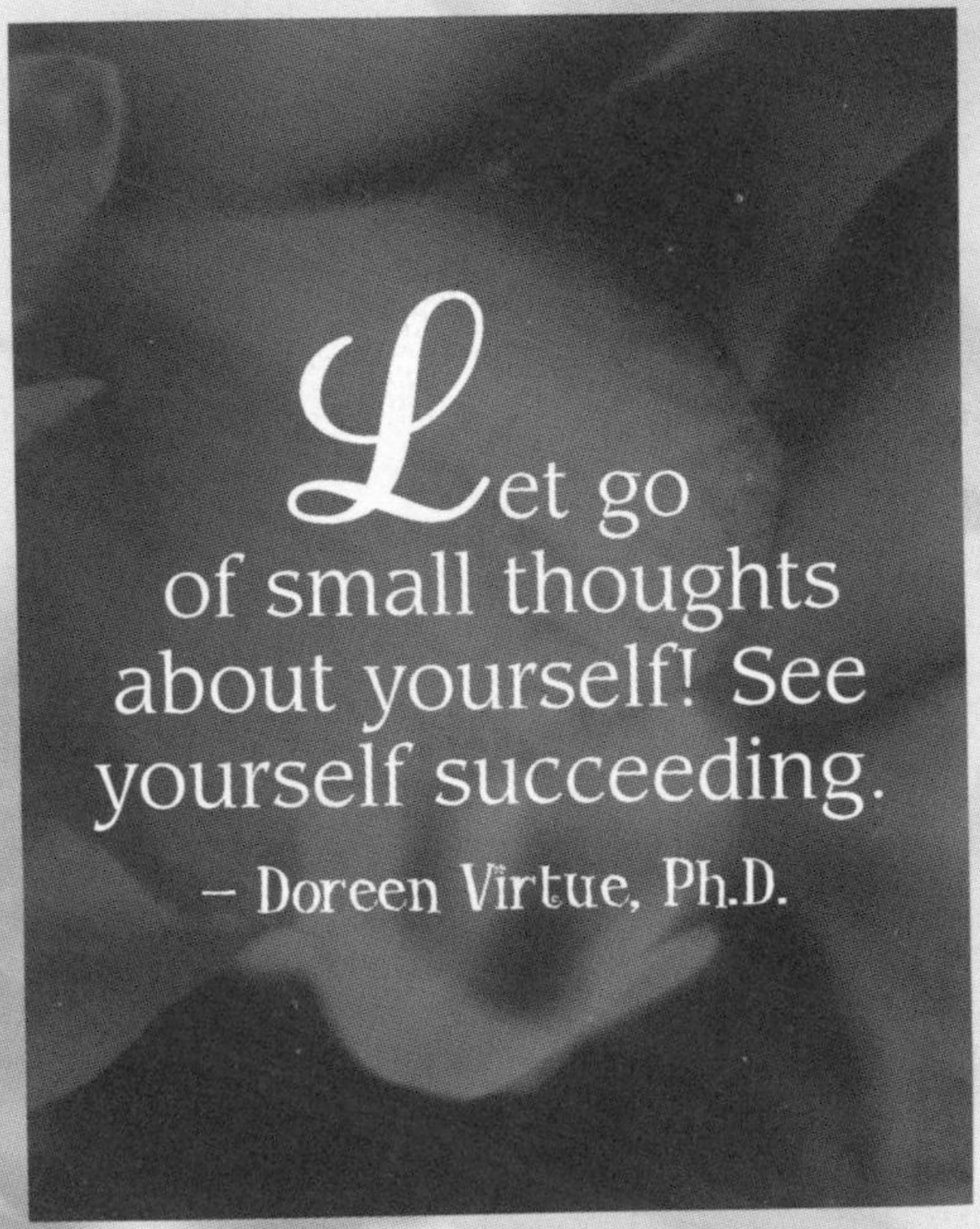
Let go
of small thoughts
about yourself! See
yourself succeeding.
– Doreen Virtue, Ph.D.

Make time to relax, be still, and enjoy your solitude, indulging in much-needed self-care.

– Doreen Virtue, Ph.D.

When you surrender and let go of the past, you allow yourself to be fully alive in the moment. Letting go of the past means that you can enjoy the dream that is happening right now.

– DON Miguel Ruiz

Take the responsibility to make new agreements with those you love. If an agreement doesn't work, change that agreement and create a new one. Use your imagination to explore the possibilities.

— DON Miguel Ruiz

Here's a task: Be the bearer of only good news today. In living out this task, note whether you find it difficult to maintain. And if so, discover why within yourself.

– Caroline Myss
and Peter Occhiogrosso

Forgive one person today. Open your heart to that person, and release unnecessary suffering from the past. Feel the peace that follows from this simple act.

– Caroline Myss
and Peter Occhiogrosso

You can only control your reactions and attitudes to what happens to you. You cannot control the actual events. Learn the difference.

– Brian L. Weiss, M.D.

Love is
the energy from
which all people and
things are made.
You are connected
to everything in your
world through love.

-- Brian L. Weiss, M.D.

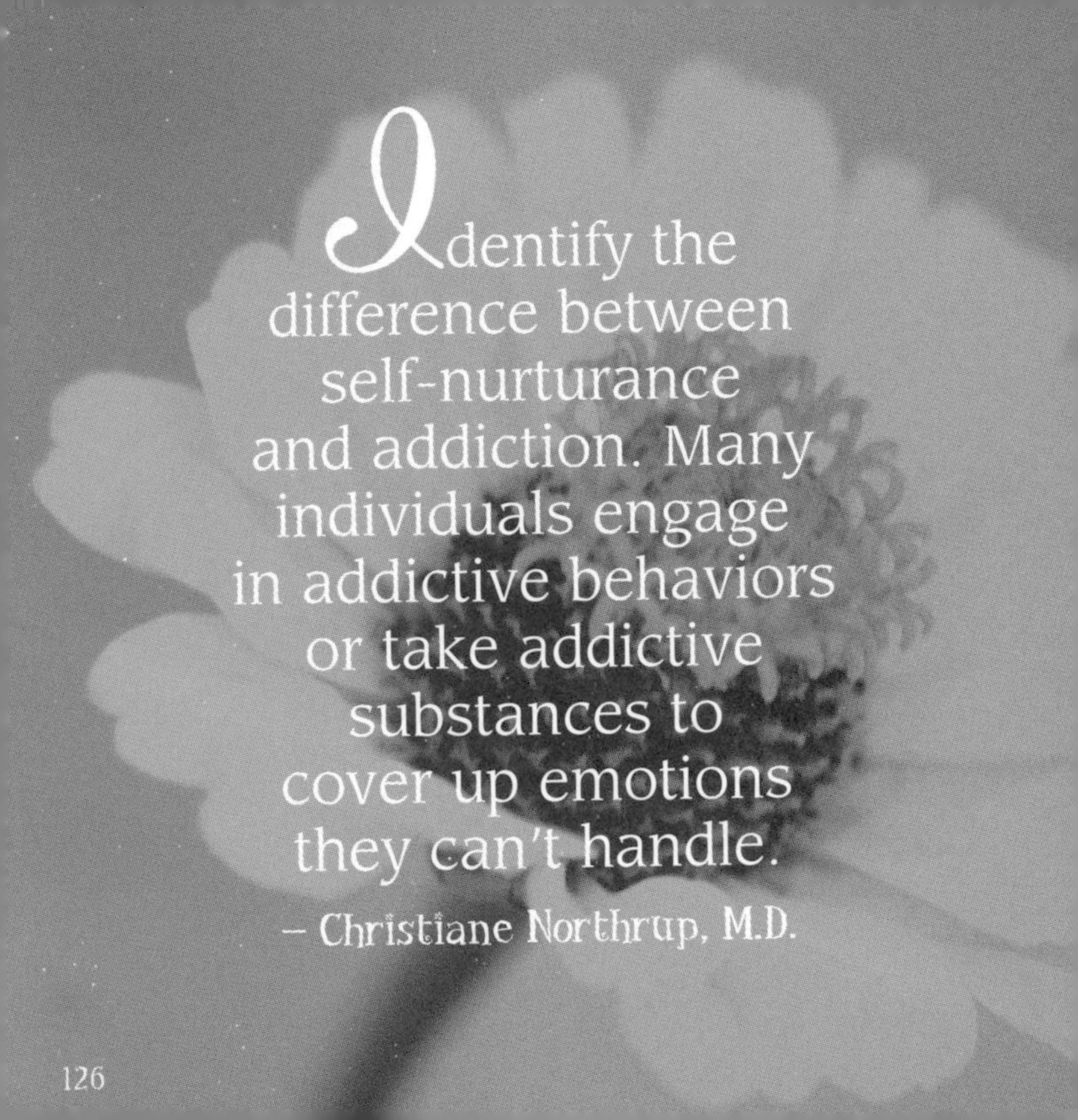

Identify the difference between self-nurturance and addiction. Many individuals engage in addictive behaviors or take addictive substances to cover up emotions they can't handle.

– Christiane Northrup, M.D.

Take yourself
and your creative
life seriously.
Make time for
self-expression.
Be disciplined.
This is the way
to develop your
unique gifts
and talents.

– Christiane Northrup, M.D.

There are two kinds of people in the world: those who pull you up and those who pull you down. Identify the people who pull you up and show them an attitude of gratitude.

– Keith D. Harrell

Empowering beliefs strengthen you. Today, create and focus on three empowering beliefs that contribute to your positive attitude.

– Keith D. Harrell

Care for your body. Self-love and self-acceptance are the ultimate acts of self-care.

– Cheryl Richardson

Set a goal, write it down, and release the outcome. Small steps make a big difference.

– Cheryl Richardson

Once you realize what God's invisible hand is doing in your life—and you then respond positively—you'll begin to flourish right away. And you'll wonder why you settled for so little for so long.

– Dr. Bruce Wilkinson

You'll make a huge spiritual leap forward when you begin to focus less on beating temptation and more on avoiding it.

– Dr. Bruce Wilkinson

How do you allow others to violate your boundaries? Are you willing to secure your boundaries today? Boundaries can only keep you safe if you let others know that they exist.

– Iyanla Vanzant

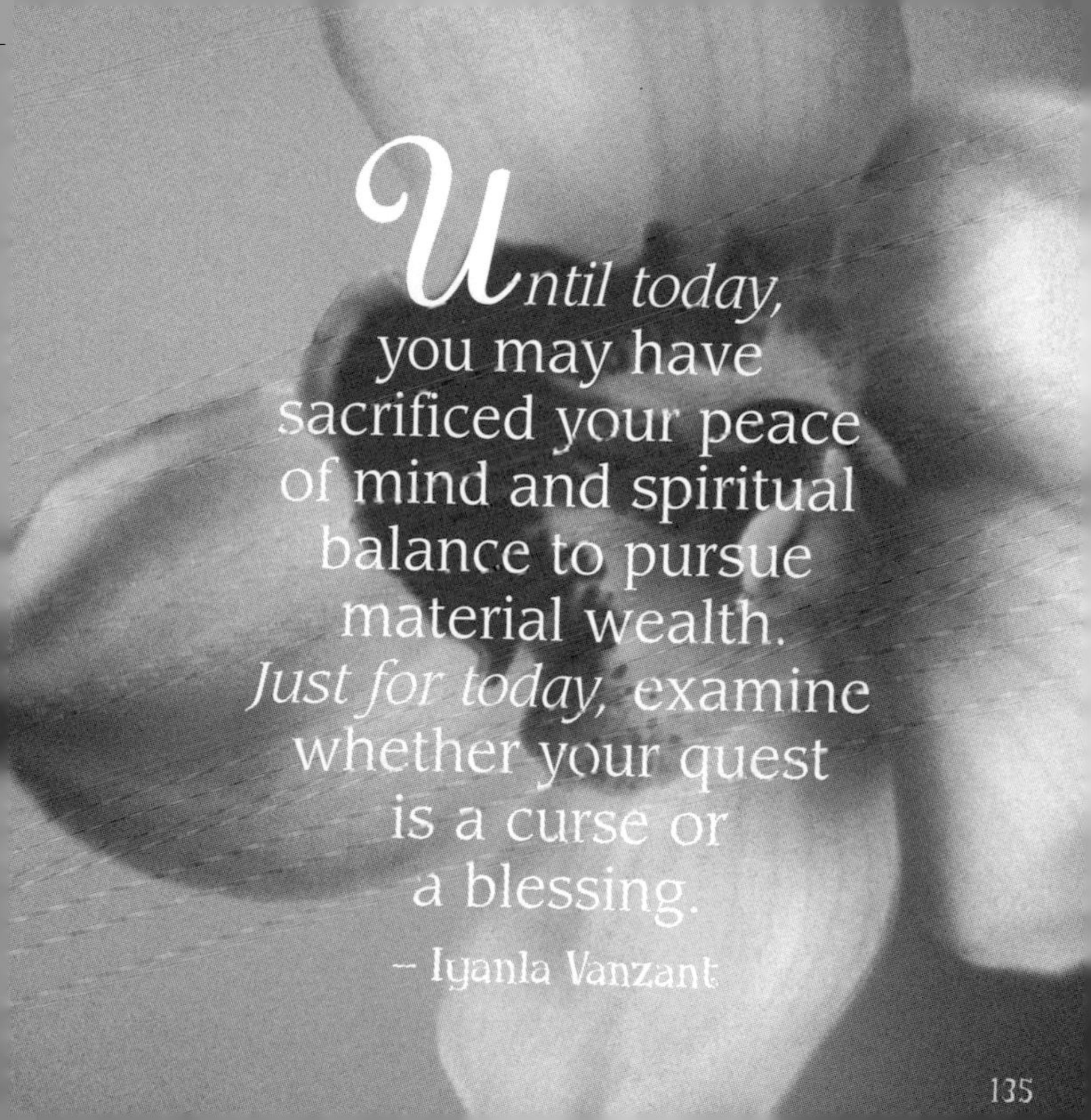

Until today, you may have sacrificed your peace of mind and spiritual balance to pursue material wealth. *Just for today,* examine whether your quest is a curse or a blessing.

– Iyanla Vanzant

When you accept the fact that the only constant is change, you'll no longer be willing to do damage to yourself and others by refusing to accept it. Welcoming change is welcoming life.

– Anne Wilson Schaef

When your children don't fit in to your fantasies of who you thought they should and would be, it could be a compliment to you.

– Anne Wilson Schaef

A woman's sense of self is defined through her feelings and the quality of her relationships. A man's sense of self is defined through his ability to achieve results.

– John Gray

Women thrive on communication because it nurtures their female side. Men thrive on appreciation because it nurtures their male side.

– John Gray

Give yourself rewards for getting through various stages of a project. Treat yourself to a movie, call a friend, or go for a walk.

– Julie Morgenstern

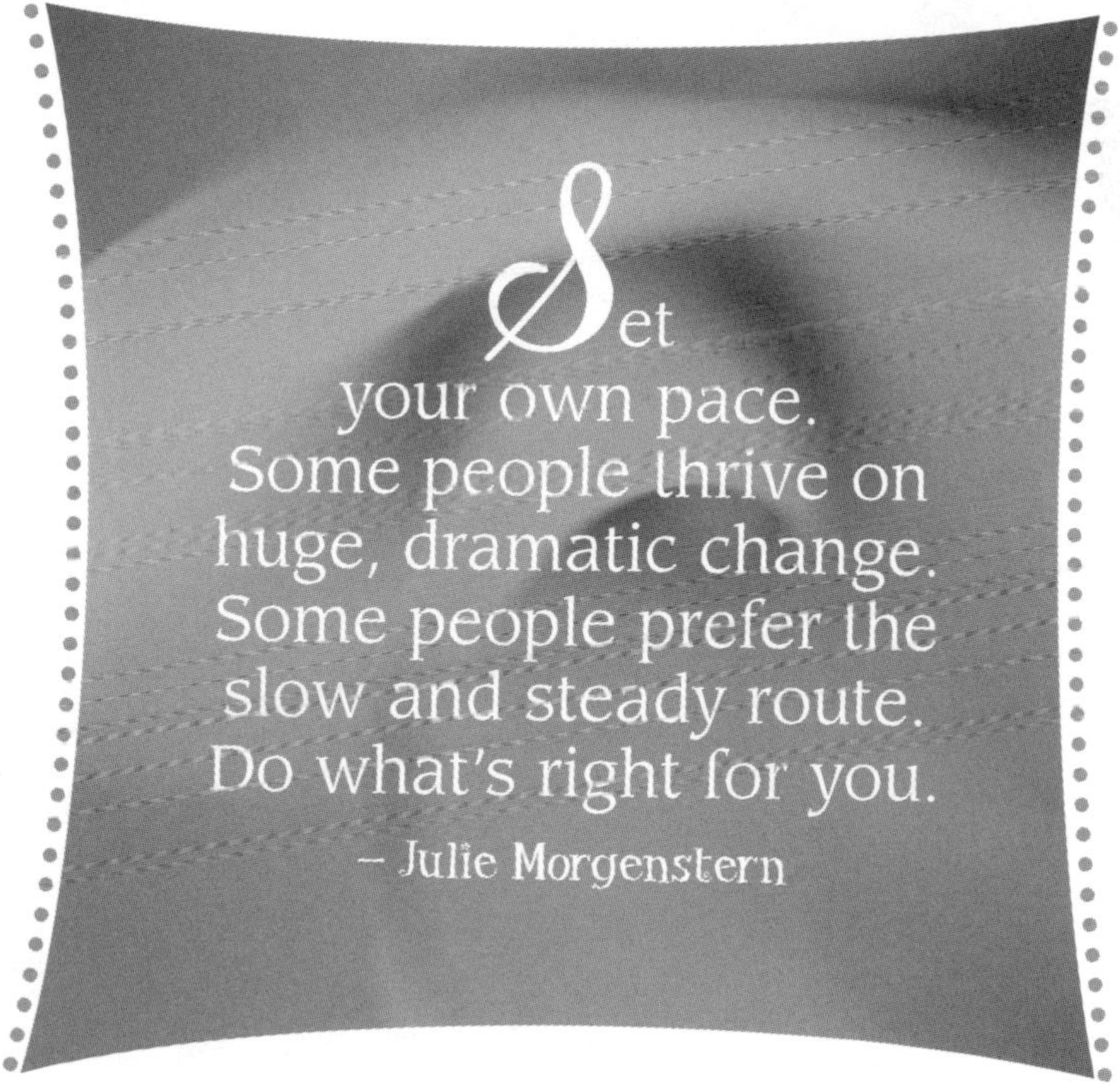
Set
your own pace.
Some people thrive on
huge, dramatic change.
Some people prefer the
slow and steady route.
Do what's right for you.
– Julie Morgenstern

God will do the right thing at the right time. And what a difference that makes! Since you know that His provision is timely, you can enjoy the present.

– Max Lucado

Demanding respect is like chasing a butterfly. Chase it, and you'll never catch it. Sit still, and it may light on your shoulder.

– Max Lucado

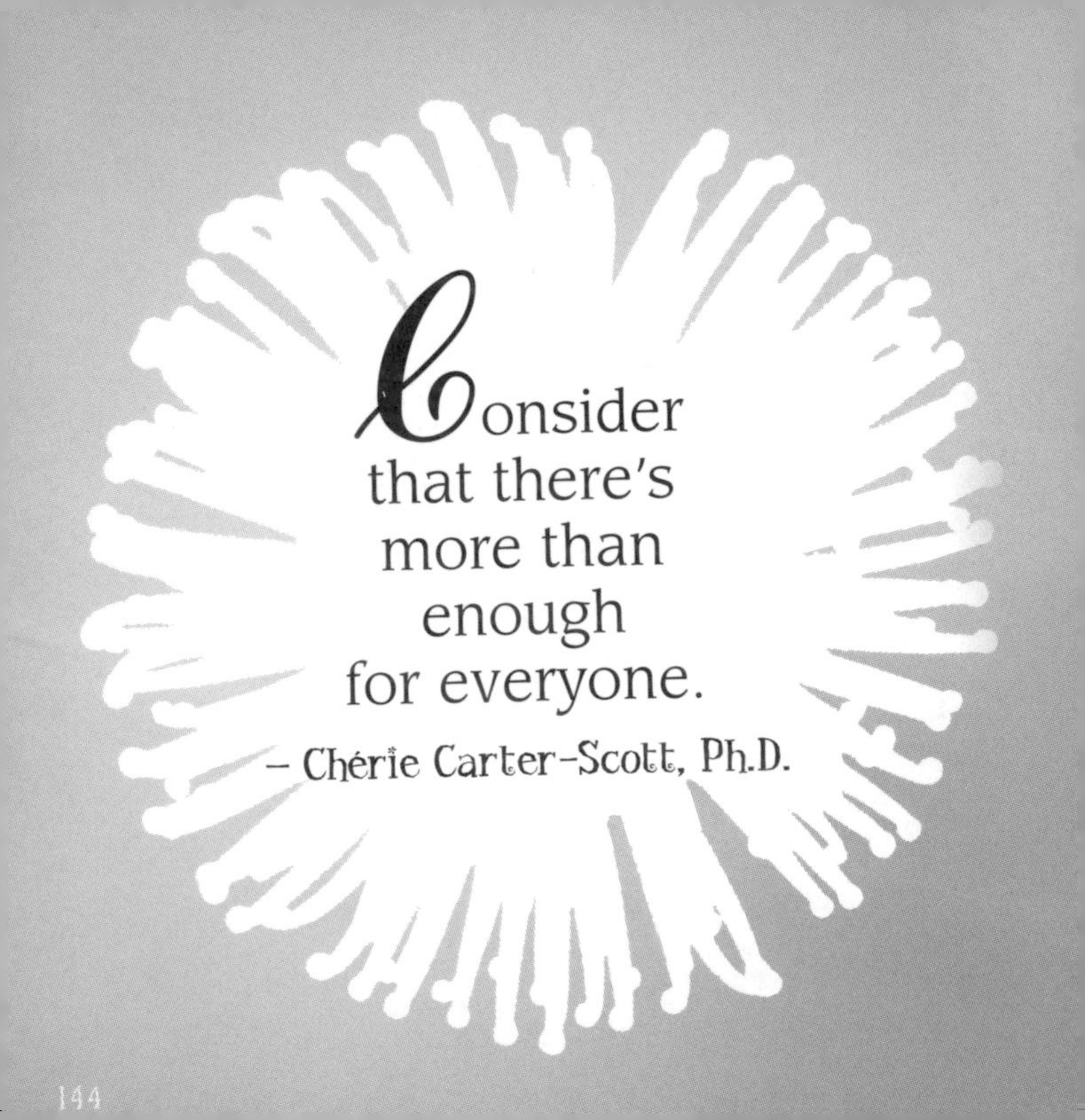
Consider
that there's
more than
enough
for everyone.
– Chérie Carter-Scott, Ph.D.

Access your highest and deepest degree of knowledge, insight, and understanding.

– Chérie Carter-Scott, Ph.D.

If you wait until you become perfect before you love yourself, you'll waste your whole life. You're already perfect right here and right now.

– Louise L. Hay

We are
all students
and teachers.
Ask yourself:
"What did I come
here to learn,
and what did
I come here
to teach?"

– Louise L. Hay

Everything you are against can be restated in a way that puts you in *support* of something. Instead of being at war, be at *peace*; instead of being against poverty, be *for* prosperity.

– Dr. Wayne W. Dyer

If you don't love yourself, nobody else will. Not only that—you won't be good at loving anyone else. Loving starts with the self.

– Dr. Wayne W. Dyer

Lies corrupt the soul. When you lie, you not only deceive someone else, you fool yourself as well. Spirituality is found in truth.

– Sylvia Browne

Treat your body with respect by feeding it nourishing and nutritious foods. If you're good to your body, it will be good to you.

– Sylvia Browne

When you recognize that your emotions, as well as others', can be capricious at times, you are better able to forgive and forget.

– Deepak Chopra, M.D.

Good luck happens when an opportunity presents itself. Meet it with preparedness.

– Deepak Chopra, M.D.

Your financial life is like a garden. If you tend a garden carefully—nourishing the flowers, pruning and weeding—it's going to be a lot more beautiful than if you simply water it halfheartedly now and then.

– Suze Orman

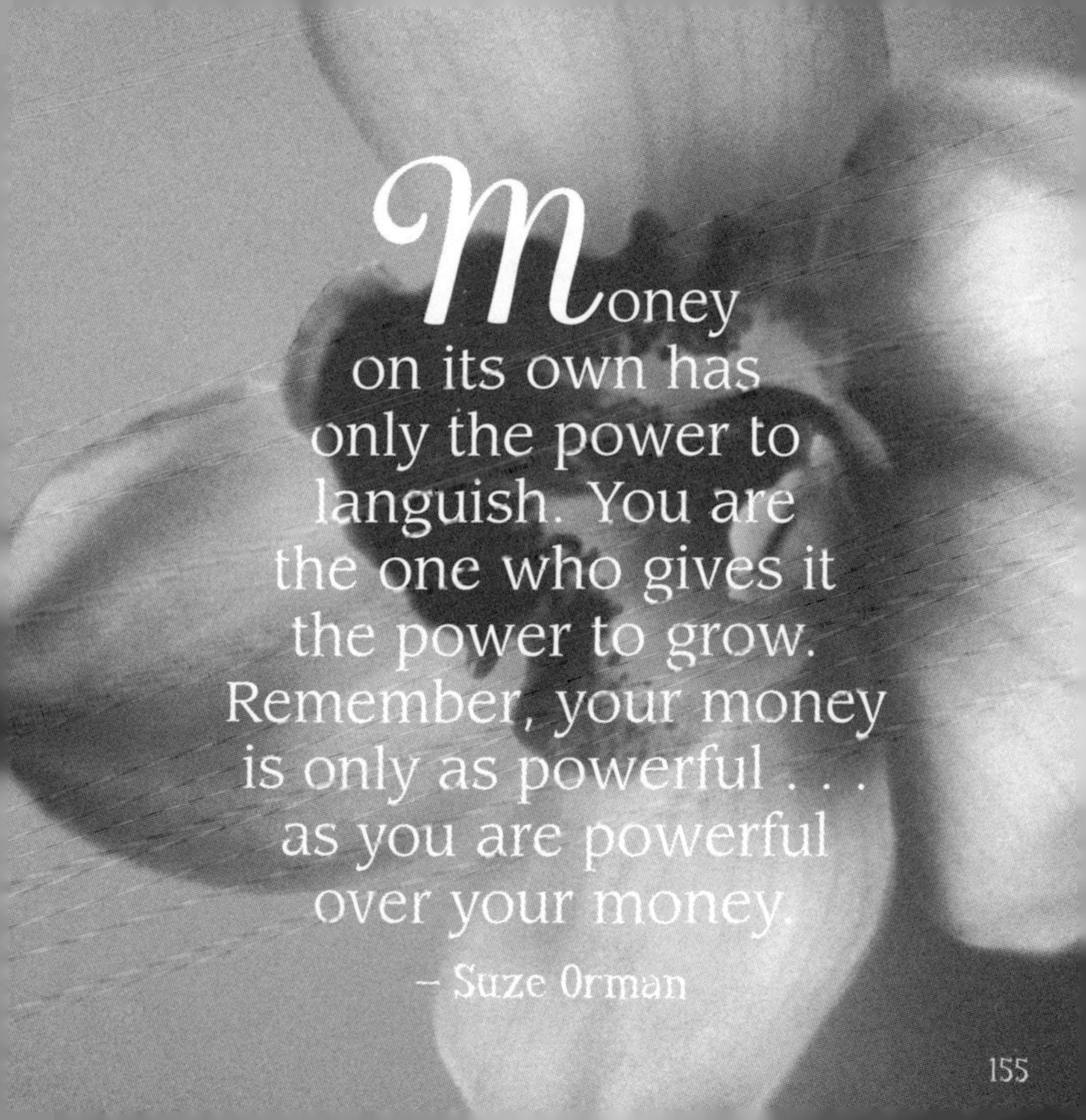

Money on its own has only the power to languish. You are the one who gives it the power to grow. Remember, your money is only as powerful . . . as you are powerful over your money.

– Suze Orman

You are your word. Say what you will do, and do what you say. Never call your word into question with lies, deceit, or misrepresentation. Create credibility by honoring your word.

– Tavis Smiley

Know that everything you do comes back to you. Step outside yourself and consider the consequence before you make a move. If your action will bring peace to yourself and others, it's the right thing to do.

– Tavis Smiley

Your generosity toward others is key to your positive experiences in the world. Know that there's enough room for everyone to be passionate, creative, and successful. In fact, there's more than *room* for everyone; there's a *need* for everyone.

– Marianne Williamson

No matter what the illness or addiction or distorted physical expression, its cause is in the mind, and only there can it be healed. The greatest power you're given by God is the power to change your mind.

– Marianne Williamson

Decide what your highest priorities are, and have the courage and independent willpower to say no—pleasantly, smilingly, and unapologetically—to the things that are less important to you.

– Stephen R. Covey

Meditate, engage in daily prayers, read uplifting books, commune with Mother Nature—in some way try to remove yourself from the discord of the everyday world that invades your sense of inner peace.

– Stephen R. Covey

Selfishly seek joy, because your joy is the greatest gift you can give to anyone. Unless you are in your joy, you have nothing to give anyway.

– Abraham-Hicks

You are
not here to fix anything,
because nothing is
broken, but everything
is continually changing
and expanding.
Release your struggle,
and seek joy and fun,
and in doing so, you
will align with the
fantastic expanding
rhythm of this Universe.

– Abraham-Hicks

Allow others to give you loving care. Receive without guilt or apologies.

– Doreen Virtue, Ph.D.

Say positive affirmations each morning to open the gates of manifestation.

-- Doreen Virtue, Ph.D.

Find the courage to ask for what you want. Others have the right to tell you yes or no, but you always have the right to ask. Likewise, everybody has the right to ask you for what they want, and you have the right to say yes or no.

— DON Miguel Ruiz

The supreme act of forgiveness is when you can forgive yourself for all the wounds you've created in your own life. Forgiveness is an act of self-love. When you forgive yourself, self-acceptance begins and self-love grows.

— DON Miguel Ruiz

We often blind ourselves to beauty precisely because it inspires us to go beyond ourselves. Today, find only beauty, especially when your first instinct is to be critical of someone, something, or some opportunity.

– Caroline Myss
and Peter Occhiogrosso

Ask yourself, "What are my desires?" Then ask, "What are my genuine needs?" Discover how casually you desire things that have no real value for you. Then you'll realize how easily you lose your power.

– Caroline Myss and Peter Occhiogrosso

To reach out with love, to do your best and not be so concerned with results or outcomes—that's the way to live.

– Brian L. Weiss, M.D.

In this world, you learn through relationships, not things. You can't take your things with you when you leave.

-- Brian L. Weiss, M.D.

Become a lifelong learner. Expose yourself to new ideas. Take classes regularly. Resolve to remain teachable throughout your life.

– Christiane Northrup, M.D.

Your surroundings, home, personal care, pets, clothing, and body are all reflections of how you see and express yourself. Do these reflect your true self?

– Christiane Northrup, M.D.

Goals are tools for focusing on your life and for inspiring you to take action. Today, determine the worth of your goals . . . because everything you want may not actually be worth having.

– Keith D. Harrell

What *has* happened is not nearly as important as what *can* happen. Look to the possibilities of your future for direction, forsaking the burdensome limitations of your past.

– Keith D. Harrell

Have
a good cry.
Grief is a
doorway to
your deepest self.

– Cheryl Richardson

Schedule
a sacred date
with yourself.
You deserve time
for *your* life.

– Cheryl Richardson

Stand
firm in knowing
that God has already
prepared a significant
life for you that
He will faithfully
bring into being.

– Dr. Bruce Wilkinson

Reach boldly
for the miracle.
God knows
your gifts,
your hindrances,
and the condition
you're in at
every moment.

– Dr. Bruce Wilkinson

Who needs to hear "I apologize" from you? Are you willing to apologize to someone today? An apology is not an admission of guilt or wrongdoing. It's an acknowledgment that you're willing to do better next time.

– Iyanla Vanzant

Until today, you may have made excuses for the unkempt and incomplete areas in your life. *Just for today,* be devoted to acknowledging the things you've left undone, unsaid, and incomplete. Acknowledgment is the first step toward healing.

– Iyanla Vanzant

Dear one,
who is it you will
not talk to?
Who is it you
will not forgive,
dead or alive?
It is time for closure!

– Kryon

Take
the word *victim*
off of your person—
out of your vocabulary.
It reeks with the
old energy and
does not suit your
magnificence.

– Kryon

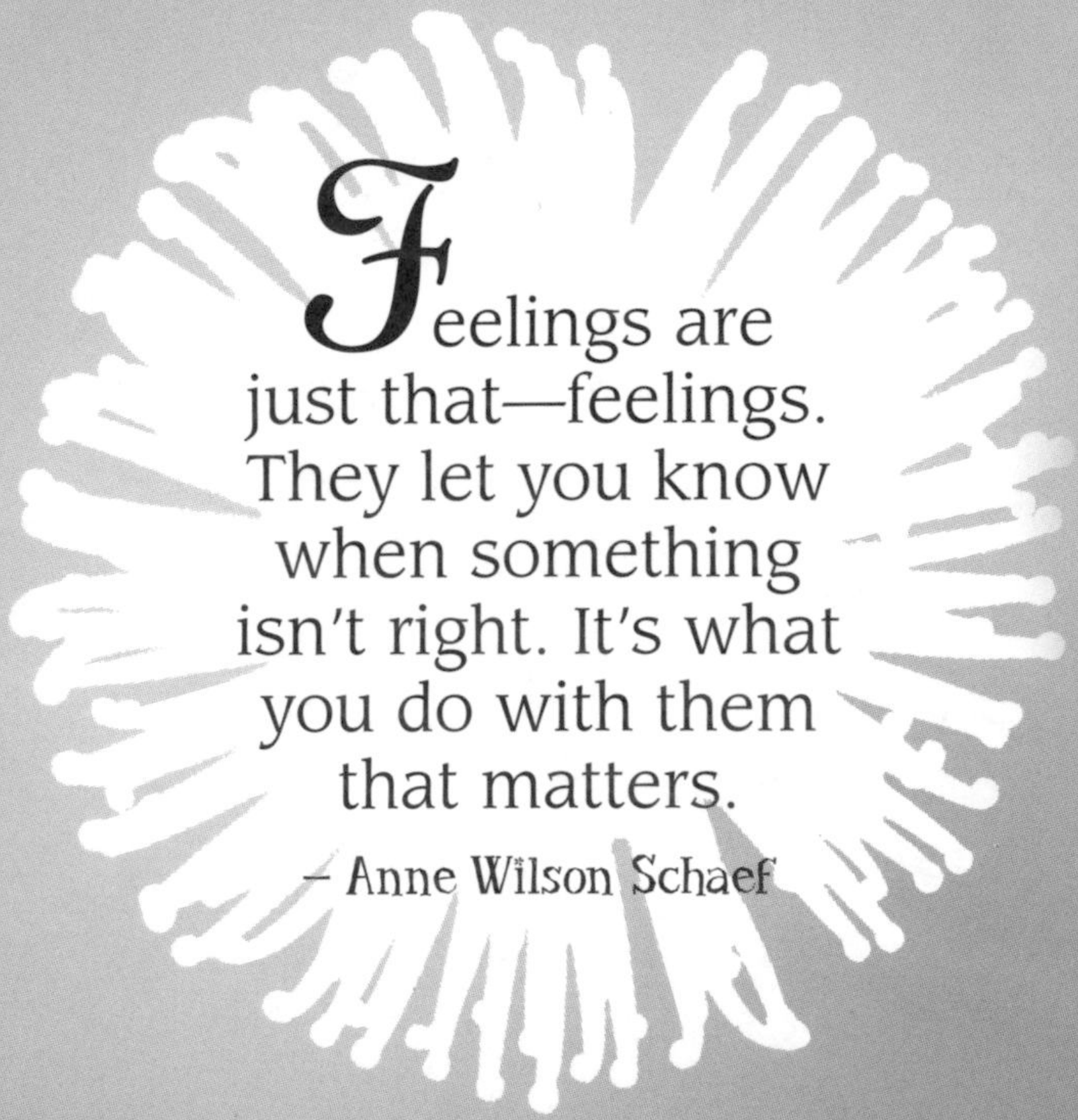

Feelings are just that—feelings. They let you know when something isn't right. It's what you do with them that matters.

– Anne Wilson Schaef

Good communication is a balance of speaking and sharing, listening carefully and absorbing . . . before you speak again.

– Anne Wilson Schaef

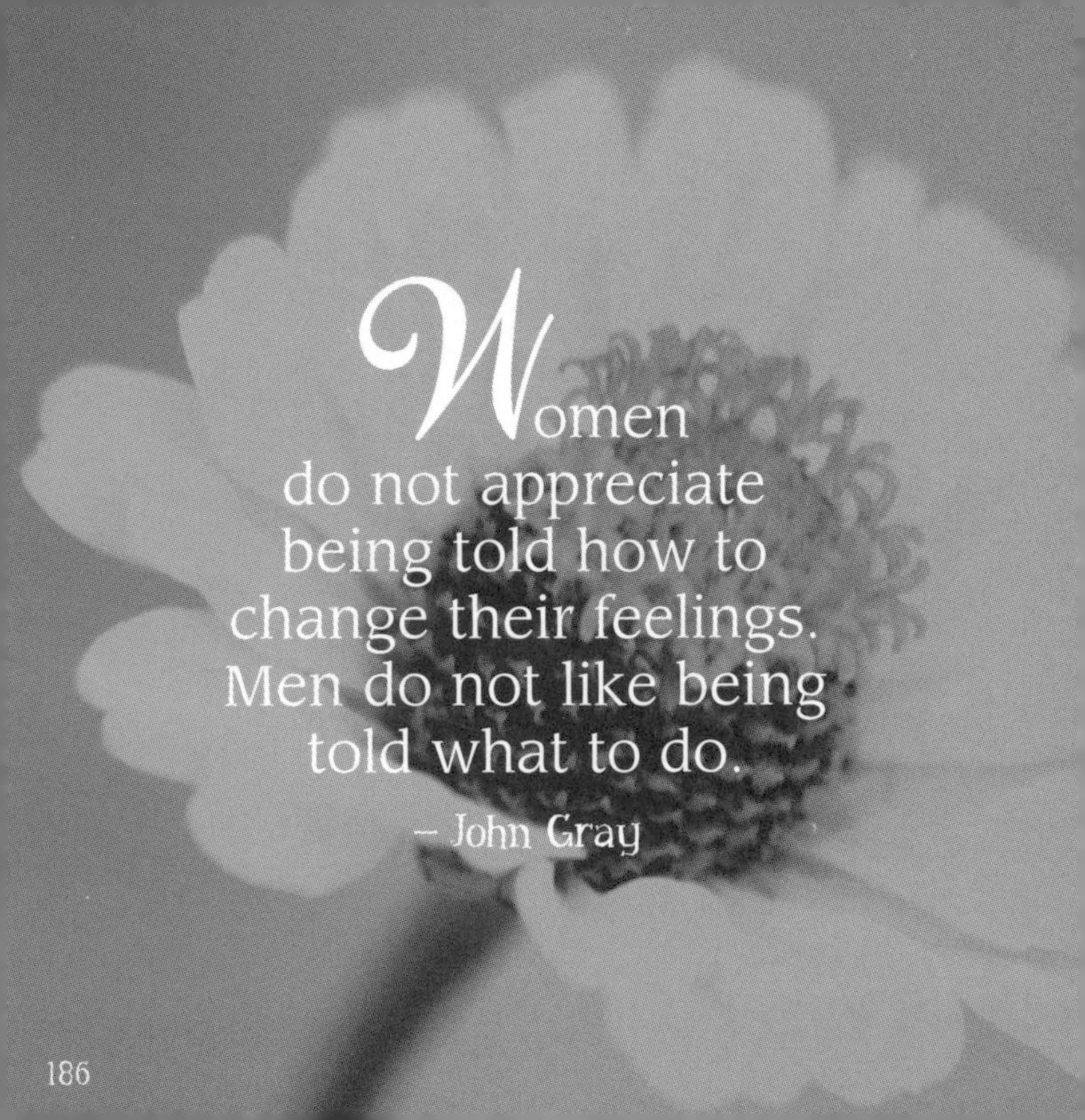

Women do not appreciate being told how to change their feelings. Men do not like being told what to do.

– John Gray

The more a woman feels the right to be upset, the less upset she will be. When men talk about their problems, they're looking for solutions.

– John Gray

If you feel happier surrounded by a lot of stuff, then don't try to create a spare, streamlined environment. Instead, enjoy your possessions by organizing them.

– Julie Morgenstern

Are your closets, drawers, and cabinets filled up with things that you never use? Get rid of the excess to make room for what you love.

– Julie Morgenstern

Don't face death without facing God. Don't even speak of death without speaking to God. He and He alone can guide you through the valley. And only God is committed to getting you there safely.

– Max Lucado

Be specific with your prayers. Give God the number of the flight. Tell Him the length of the speech. Share the details of the job transfer. He has plenty of time and compassion. He doesn't think your fears are foolish or silly. He's been where you are. He knows how you feel. And He knows what you need.

– Max Lucado

As your understanding of life continues to grow, you can walk upon this planet safe and secure, always moving forward toward your greater good.

– Louise L. Hay

You cannot learn other people's lessons for them. They must do the work themselves, and they'll do it when they're ready.

– Louise L. Hay

Forgiveness is the most powerful thing you can do for yourself on the spiritual path. If you can't learn to forgive, you can forget about getting to higher levels of awareness.

– Dr. Wayne W. Dyer

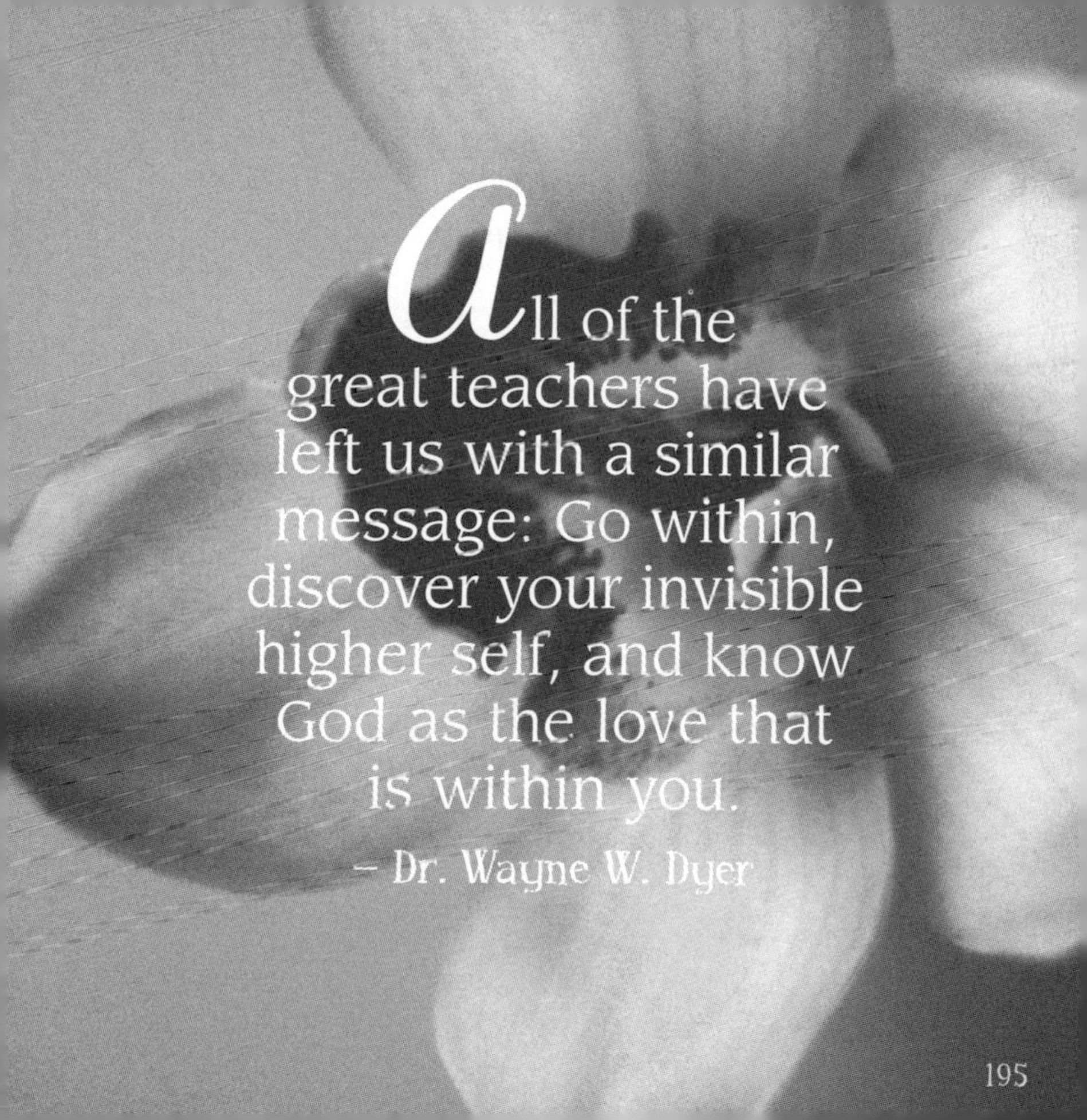

All of the great teachers have left us with a similar message: Go within, discover your invisible higher self, and know God as the love that is within you.

– Dr. Wayne W. Dyer

Patience truly is a virtue, and it is one attribute that we all have to perfect in one form or another. Instead of getting impatient, try doing a short meditation—breathe deeply and think pleasant thoughts.

– Sylvia Browne

Whether due to death or divorce, the loss of a loved one leaves a horrendous hole behind. The only way to achieve wellness is to "get out of yourself" by immediately helping others.

– Sylvia Browne

Recognize that when you're in balance, you possess a level of strength and flexibility that allows you to meet any challenge effortlessly.

– Deepak Chopra, M.D.

If you can learn from every relationship and understand how it came into your life, then no relationship needs to be remembered with regret.

– Deepak Chopra, M.D.

Have the courage to discuss your financial situation with your partner out of love, not greed—out of wanting the best for each other—not only now, but forever. Then no matter what happens, you have nothing to lose.

– Suze Orman

How much money is enough? For each and every one of us, that amount is different, unique as a fingerprint. Seek and celebrate all that you can create, then you will have all that you're meant to have. That will be enough.

– Suze Orman

Each obstacle you overcome is a stepping-stone on your path to greatness. Appreciate the obstacle, for it empowers you to courageously face future barriers in your quest for success.

– Tavis Smiley

Put your heart into everything you do. A lukewarm effort produces mediocre results. Pour on the passion, and experience intense success in all your achievements.

– Tavis Smiley

With your own kids, you have the chance to rewrite history—to parent them as you wish you had been parented. Thus does your own re-parenting occur. You release the future as you release the past.

– Marianne Williamson

Heaven is within you. It has nothing to do with the thoughts of someone else, and everything to do with what you yourself choose to think. Forgiving everyone is your ticket to heaven, and your only way Home. May you learn to think as God thinks.

– Marianne Williamson

Learn to delegate responsibility. Transferring responsibility to other skilled and trained people enables you to devote your energy to other high-leverage activities. Delegation means growth, both for individuals and organizations.

– Stephen R. Covey

By focusing on relationships and results rather than time and methods, you can become a listener, a trainer, and a consultant to those in your sphere of influence. Your effectiveness—and that of those around you—will increase dramatically.

– Stephen R. Covey

If the way you feel depends on anything outside of you, you're in trouble—but if you depend only upon your connection with your own Inner Being, then everything in your experience falls into alignment.

– Abraham-Hicks

Whatever you desire--and then allow--you must experience. There is no exception to that. As you hold yourself in vibrational alignment with your own desire, you will experience, in all ways, the fulfillment of that desire.

– Abraham-Hicks

Let go of old guilt, and remember that you're God's perfect child!

– Doreen Virtue, Ph.D.

Notice repetitious signs and your inner guidance, as this can yield valuable information.

– Doreen Virtue, Ph.D.

Your *body* is a living temple where God lives. Your *mind* is a living temple where God lives. God is living within you as Life. The proof that God lives within you is that you are alive. Your *Life* is the proof.

– DON Miguel Ruiz

All the magic you possess is based on your word, and you cast spells all the time with your opinions. You can either put a spell on someone with your word, or you can release someone from a spell.

— DON Miguel Ruiz

a visit or a call from a friend can heal you. You can also heal a friend in this same way. Is there someone you've been wanting to contact but haven't made time for? Today, make the time.

– Caroline Myss
and Peter Occhiogrosso

Help others quietly, without expecting gratitude or rewards. Let the healing power of your spirit run through your hand as you reach to touch another, but say nothing to the person you help. Learn to give invisibly.

– Caroline Myss
and Peter Occhiogrosso

If you're evolving into a more loving, more compassionate, less violent person, then you're moving in the right direction.

– Brian L. Weiss, M.D.

It's better to speak from your heart with everyone you communicate with. Otherwise, anger will creep in, and you'll resent the person or the obligation.

– Brian L. Weiss, M.D.

Know when to take action to change or leave a partnership. Know when to allow it to remain as is. In a true partnership, each member is free to leave.

– Christiane Northrup, M.D.

All creations need care and feeding. Water and fertilize your creations and dreams with positive, uplifting emotions, thoughts, and love.

– Christiane Northrup, M.D.

There's
no statute of
limitations on
forgiveness.
In the presence
or absence of
explanation,
forgive yourself
and forgive others.

– Keith D. Harrell

Smile and
laugh often!
Each day,
find something
happy, joyful,
and funny about life—
smile and laugh,
smile and laugh, and
smile and laugh again.

– Keith D. Harrell

Think BIG.
There are
unseen forces
ready to support
your dreams.

– Cheryl Richardson

Connect
with someone special.
A loved one
is a gift to treasure.

– Cheryl Richardson

God's actions are all intended to nudge you—lovingly, wisely, persistently—toward the life and character you desire but can't reach without help.

– Dr. Bruce Wilkinson

Be assured that, at the right time, God will provide you with the right words to say and a boldness to say them that you never thought possible.

– Dr. Bruce Wilkinson

How can you bring some excitement into your life? Are you willing to experience excitement today? Excitement is the result of doing the very thing you've convinced yourself you can't do!

– Iyanla Vanzant

Until today, you may have been holding on to something or someone, not realizing that its purpose in your life has been served. *Just for today,* surrender all attachments to the people and things you've been struggling to hold on to.

– Iyanla Vanzant

Develop
an unshakable
allegiance
to someone
or something.

– Chérie Carter-Scott, Ph.D.

Perceive things as equitable, then anticipate justice prevailing.

– Chérie Carter-Scott, Ph.D.

If you call upon the names of your beloved ones who have passed, you might be interested to know that a piece of them is with you. Part of their spiritual contract is to be with you in this way. It is the same for you when you leave the earth.

– Kryon

Visualize in your mind the perfect solution without knowing what it is! Visualize the challenge being over and being peaceful with everything around you. Don't tell Spirit how to solve it. Instead, visualize it being finished.

– Kryon

When you respect your anger and deal with it, you discover doors into your inner being that weren't obvious before.

– Anne Wilson Schaef

Giving up blaming others for your unhappiness, your perceived failures, and your life may leave you silent for a while. But the silence is worth it. It leads to clamoring awareness.

– Anne Wilson Schaef

A man's greatest challenge is to take responsibility for his contribution to a problem. A woman's greatest challenge is to let go of her resentment and find forgiveness.

– John Gray

Women love
to care for their men,
but primarily,
they need to feel
cared for themselves.
Men need to feel
cared for, but primarily,
they need to feel
successful in fulfilling
their partners.

– John Gray

Letting go of unused items can put extra cash in your pocket. Donate them for the tax deduction, or resell them at a garage sale or consignment shop.

– Julie Morgenstern

Organize your rooms. An organized room takes no more than three to five minutes to clean up, no matter how messy it gets.

– Julie Morgenstern

Bless your home with love. Put love in every corner so that your home lovingly responds with warmth and comfort. Be at peace.

– Louise L. Hay

Choose to believe that "everyone is always helpful." Therefore, wherever you go in life, people will be there to assist you.

– Louise L. Hay

When you lay your ego aside and return to that from which you originally emanated, you'll begin to immediately see the power of intention working with, for, and through you in a multitude of ways.

– Dr. Wayne W. Dyer

Every thought you have impacts you. By shifting in the middle of a weakening thought to one that strengthens, you raise your energy vibration and strengthen yourself and the immediate energy field.

– Dr. Wayne W. Dyer

Try to avoid thinking about what you're not: "I'm not happy, not rich, not good-looking," and so on. Instead, think about what you *are:*
"I am joyful;
I am prosperous;
I am beautiful."
Your self-esteem will rise immeasurably.

– Sylvia Browne

There are definitely things you should not do to excess. For example, addictions that harm your physical body stop your soul's growth and cloud your direct rapport with God. Ask God to help strengthen your will and help you learn restraint.

– Sylvia Browne

In order to create good luck in your life, it's often best to keep silent about your innermost dreams and intentions. Simply let your vision unfold naturally.

– Deepak Chopra, M.D.

How you emotionally respond in a relationship—with joy, sadness, fear, or anger—can say a lot about your thoughts and belief systems.

– Deepak Chopra, M.D.

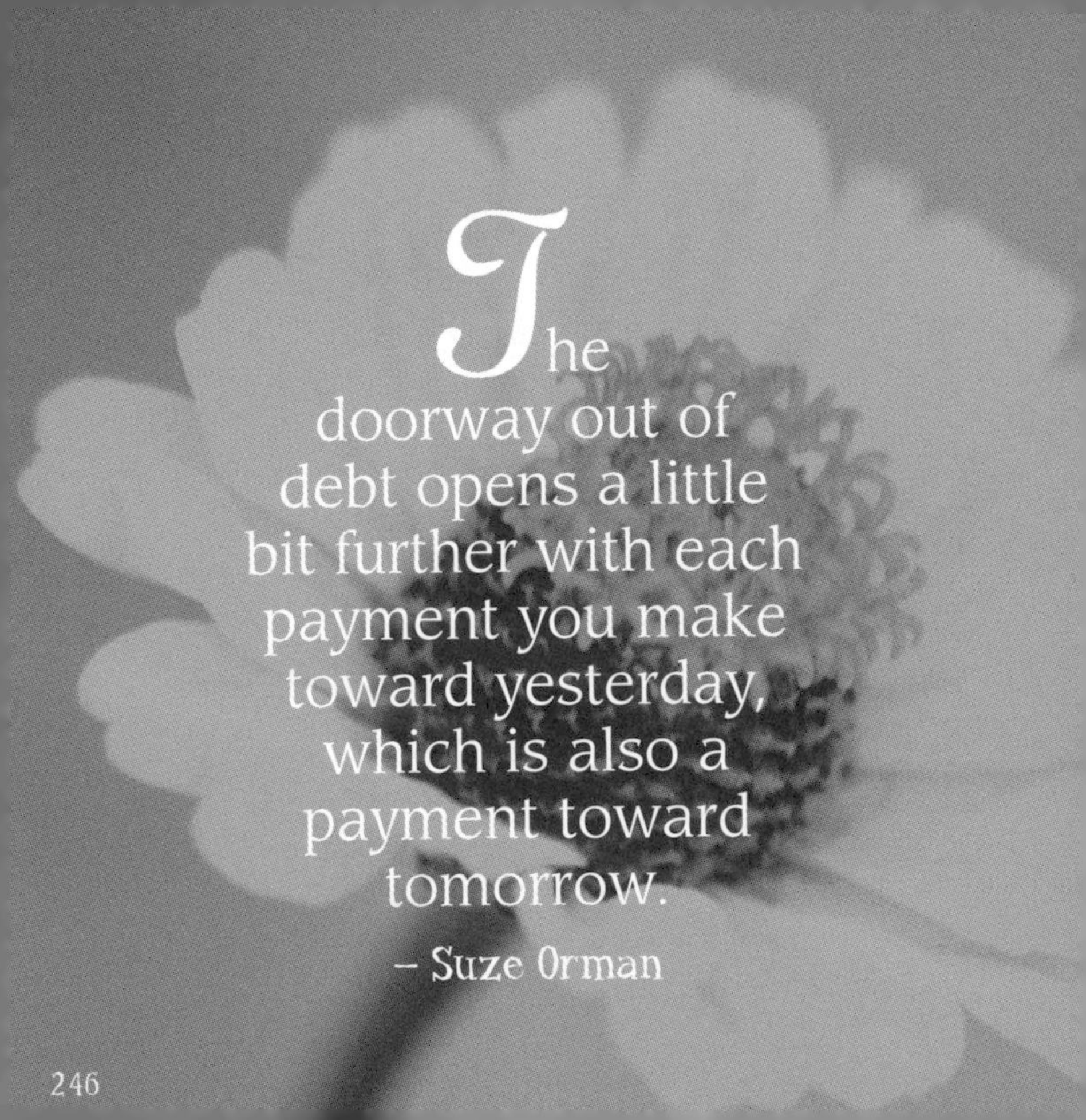

The doorway out of debt opens a little bit further with each payment you make toward yesterday, which is also a payment toward tomorrow.

– Suze Orman

One way to get in touch with your money is to actually start *touching* it again. Handle your cash; feel it and respect it; delight in spending it the way you did as a child; enjoy choosing *not* to spend it; take pleasure in putting it away now . . . for later.

– Suze Orman

You are God's divine design. He does not make mistakes. Don't get caught up in wanting to be or trying to be like someone else. Everyone is gifted in different ways. Love being you.

– Tavis Smiley

Ask how you can serve the community rather than asking how the community can serve you. When you use your calling to make a difference in the community, opportunities to create abundance will emerge in your life.

– Tavis Smiley

Meditation is a time of quiet, when the mind is freed from its attachment to the hysterical ravings of a world gone mad. It is a silence in which the spirit of God can enter us and work His divine alchemy upon us.

– Marianne Williamson

a healthy, vital society is not one in which we all agree. It is one in which those who disagree can do so with honor and respect for other people's opinions . . . and an appreciation of our shared humanity.

– Marianne Williamson

Create opportunities to interact one-on-one with your boss, your children, your spouse, your friends, and your employees. When you listen, you learn, which opens the door to creative solutions and mutual trust.

– Stephen R. Covey

Nurture your physical self by eating the right foods, getting sufficient rest and relaxation, and exercising on a regular basis. A good exercise program will build your body in three areas: endurance, flexibility, and strength.

– Stephen R. Covey

You were born with a magnificent (emotional) guidance system that lets you know, in every moment, exactly what your vibrational content is, which is being matched by the Law of Attraction. As it is your desire to feel good, and your practice to choose good-feeling thoughts, only good things will come to you.

– Abraham-Hicks

Thriving
is as natural
as breathing itself.
By relaxing often
and breathing
deeply,
your natural
thriving
is enhanced.

-- Abraham-Hicks

To manifest rapidly, think of your desire while you chant, hum, sing, or play music.

– Doreen Virtue, Ph.D.

Eliminate clutter from your home and work life to balance the flow of activities.

– Doreen Virtue, Ph.D.

The human mind is like a fertile ground where seeds are continually being planted. When you are impeccable with your word, your mind is no longer fertile ground for the words that come from fear; your mind is only fertile for the words that come from love.

— DON Miguel Ruiz

You are beautiful no matter what your mind tells you. That is a fact. If you are *aware of* your own beauty and *accept* your own beauty, the opinion of others doesn't affect you at all.

– DON Miguel Ruiz

Today is for observation. Where does your mind wander naturally—into fear or fantasy, humor or stress? Follow your mind, and observe where it goes to feed itself. Do you like what you see?

– Caroline Myss
and Peter Occhiogrosso

How much of your precious day do you invest in the past? Everything from your past except wisdom and love has long since served its purpose. Witness what calls to you from yesterday and why.

– Caroline Myss
and Peter Occhiogrosso

If you're doing the right thing, if you're not harming yourself or others, you need not be concerned with what others think. You're free!

– Brian L. Weiss, M.D.

Your true essence is your soul, which is eternal and exists in an ocean of love. You are not your body.

– Brian L. Weiss, M.D.

Cultivate a loving relationship with yourself. Be willing to be alone, and enjoy your own company.

– Christiane Northrup, M.D.

Our creations come through us freely, easily, and abundantly only when we release our need for control and allow ourselves to become clear channels for something bigger than we are.

– Christiane Northrup, M.D.

Take aim at the areas of your life that need improvement. Target three areas in your life that could use some help. Take positive action and make the necessary adjustments to reap the benefits you desire.

– Keith D. Harrell

You may realize that you see things not as they are . . . but as you think they should be. Strive to change the things in yourself that you want to change in others.

– Keith D. Harrell

Offer
your support
to someone.
Experience the joy
of serving others.

– Cheryl Richardson

Express your creativity. Delight in the mystery of your inner muse.

– Cheryl Richardson

God is at work. If you open your eyes and your mouth for Him today, you'll meet a miracle with your name written all over it.

– Dr. Bruce Wilkinson

Keep a spiritual journal of your very personal journey with God. Share with Him your disappointments, celebrations, and confusion. Ask Him for wisdom . . . and leave your request on the page until you receive guidance.

– Dr. Bruce Wilkinson

Where in your life are you offering excuses for not standing in your power? Are you ready to eliminate excuses today? Excuses are the means by which you avoid, deny, and resist the greatness you know yourself to be.

– Iyanla Vanzant

Until today, you may have been feeling overwhelmed by trying to do everything on your own. *Just for today,* ask God to help you ease some of your burdens.

– Iyanla Vanzant

Find the courage to hold on to your beliefs, even if the world around you chooses to believe differently. Have the courage to change those beliefs that no longer fit the person you have become. In doing so, you truly become yourself.

– Daniel Levin

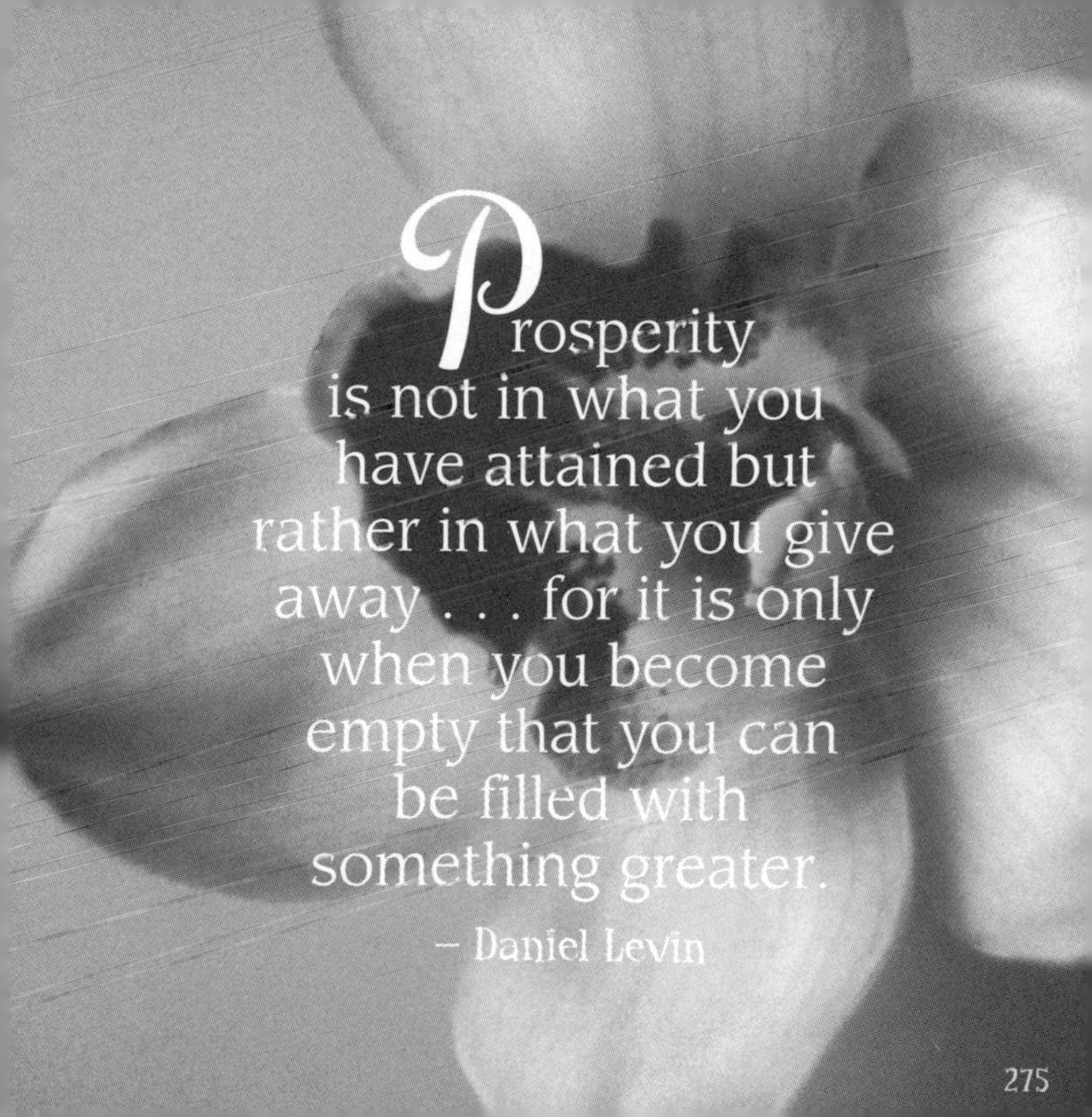

Prosperity is not in what you have attained but rather in what you give away . . . for it is only when you become empty that you can be filled with something greater.

– Daniel Levin

Be
fully in tune
with your
spiritual essence,
sustained by a
higher power.

– Chérie Carter-Scott, Ph.D.

Provide reinforcement and strength for yourself and others.

– Chérie Carter-Scott, Ph.D.

No matter what is happening around you, first take care of yourself. When you're balanced, all things will be gradually added to your life, and the changes you have asked for will occur.

– Kryon

Each time you see or hear the word *God,* think of the person next to you, the family at work or at play, and the true essence of who you are at the core. Do not think of a singular power higher than yours somewhere in the sky. It is *you!*

– Kryon

You may have believed in the past that anything worth doing was worth doing frantically. You can learn that "frantic" isn't necessary to get the job done.

– Anne Wilson Schaef

We all get discouraged at times. Just remember that growth is more like a spiral than a straight line. Discouragement is inevitable—and so is rejoicing.

– Anne Wilson Schaef

A woman expects her partner to know when she needs support. A man asks for support when he needs it.

– John Gray

Resist the temptation to solve her problems—empathize instead. Do not offer advice without being asked—just appreciate him.

-- John Gray

If you have trouble letting go of unused possessions, then adopt a charity or give them to a friend! It's easier to part with items if they're going to an organization or person you care about.

– Julie Morgenstern

Improve your quality of life. Give yourself access to the things you use and love by getting rid of the stuff you don't.

– Julie Morgenstern

Be attentive and mindful to what is happening around you at all times.

– Leon Nacson

Have
high regard for
yourself.
Be your own
best friend.

– Leon Nacson

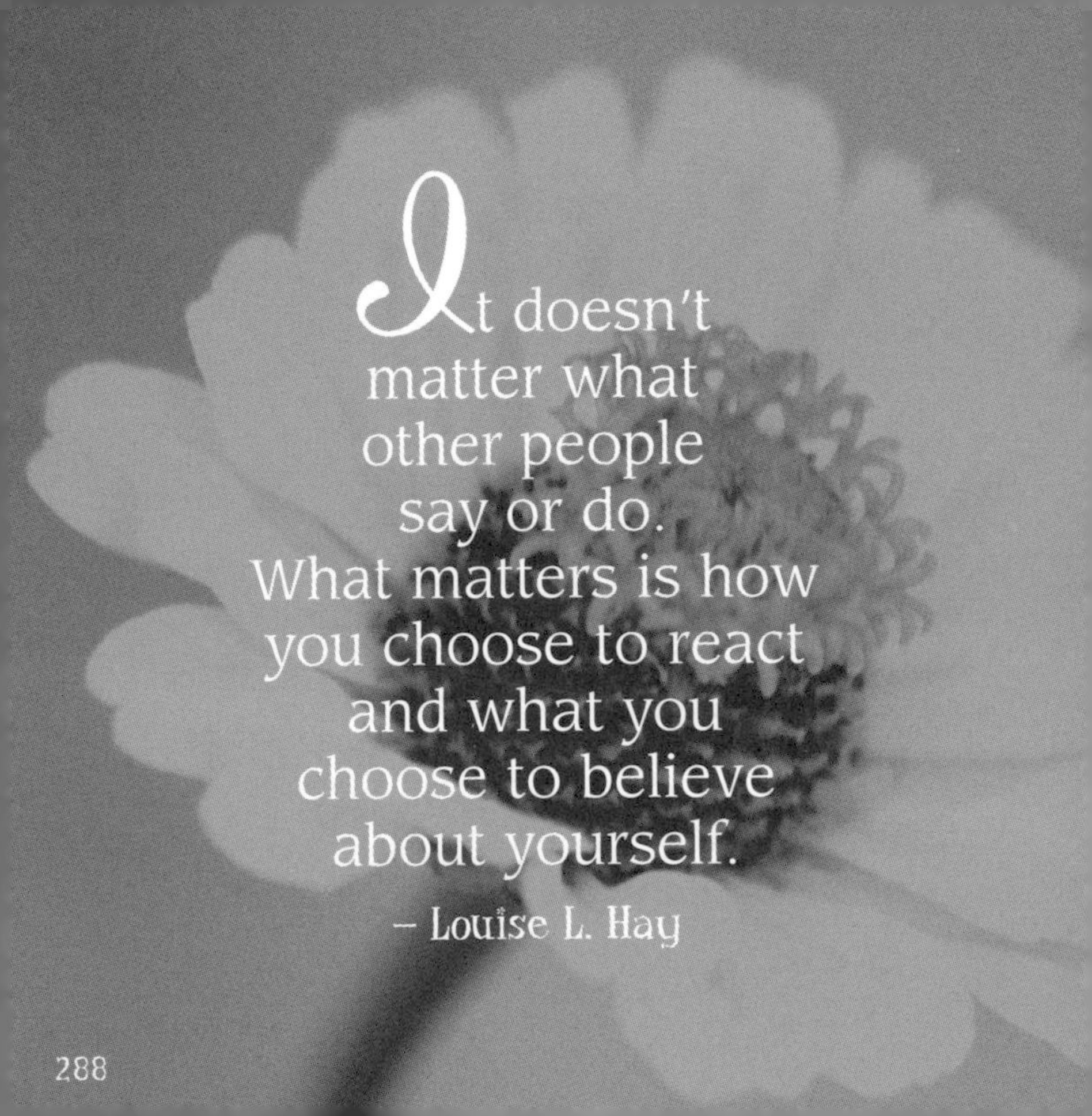

It doesn't matter what other people say or do. What matters is how you choose to react and what you choose to believe about yourself.

– Louise L. Hay

The Universe totally supports every thought you choose to think and to believe. You have unlimited choices about what to think. Choose balance, harmony, and peace, and express it in your life.

– Louise L. Hay

No one can depress you. No one can make you anxious. No one can hurt your feelings. No one can make you anything other than what you allow inside.

– Dr. Wayne W. Dyer

You can sit there forever, lamenting about how bad you've been, feeling guilty until you die, and not one tiny slice of that guilt will do anything to change the past.

– Dr. Wayne W. Dyer

Humility is a major component in being thankful, but being too humble leaves the soul in a state of feeling "not worthy." Be humble, but take pride in the fact that you have made it in life with God's grace.

– Sylvia Browne

Strength is nothing more than enduring life—to be able to survive the heartaches and agonies we go through with our heads held high. Sometimes just walking through adversity to get to the other side is a sign of strength.

– Sylvia Browne

In order to create success and money in your life, your intent and focus must be clear. You can then let the universe take care of the details.

– Deepak Chopra, M.D.

When an obstacle arises in one of your relationships, know that you can replace any fearful feelings with those of love.

– Deepak Chopra, M.D.

If you want money in your life, then you must welcome it, be open to it, and treat it with respect. Your beliefs and your attitudes are what make you feel rich and free to trust yourself, knowing that you will always take the right actions with your money.

– Suze Orman

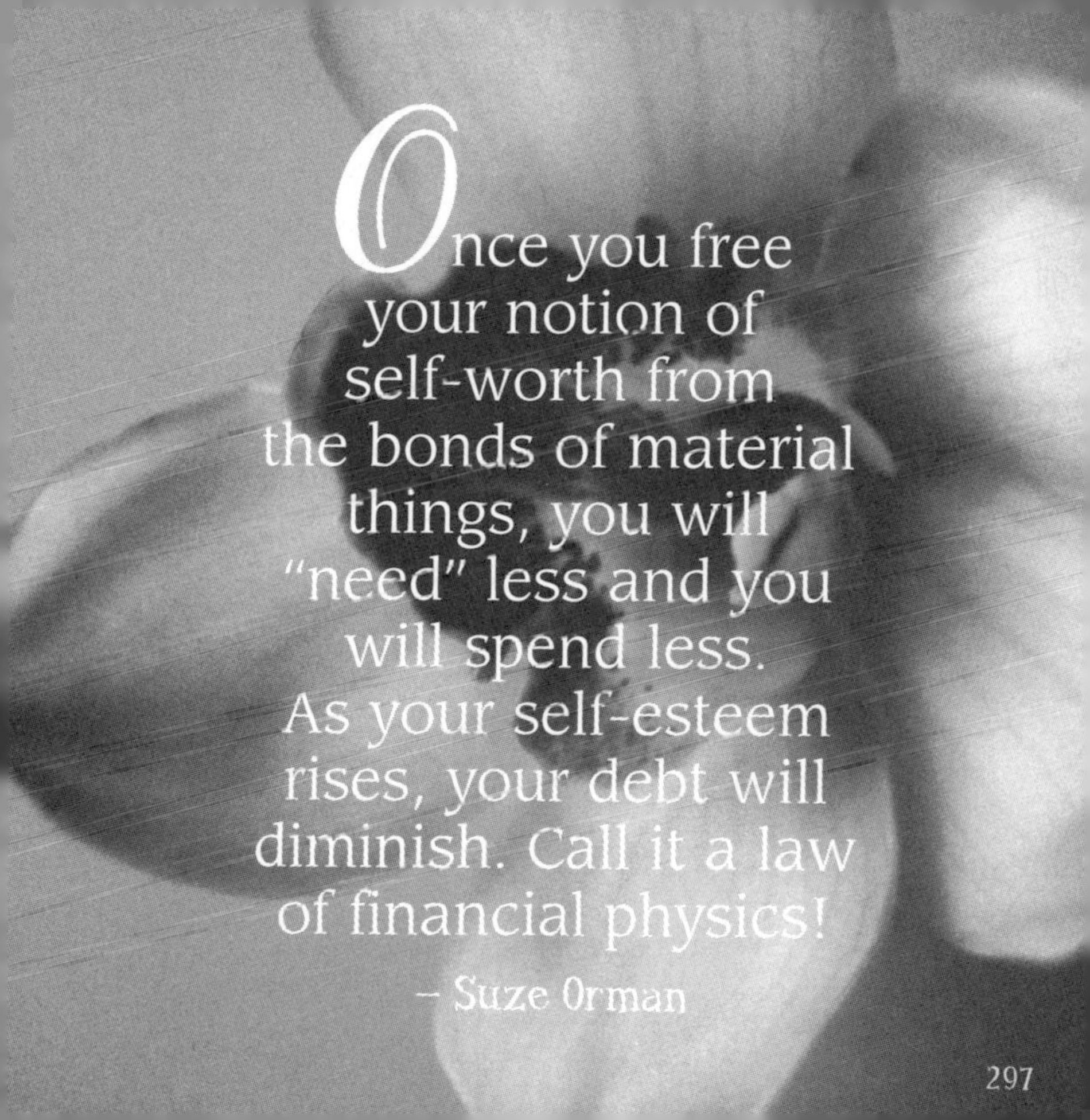

Once you free your notion of self-worth from the bonds of material things, you will "need" less and you will spend less. As your self-esteem rises, your debt will diminish. Call it a law of financial physics!

– Suze Orman

Make
others the focal point.
Give generously,
listen intently,
praise freely,
and love unceasingly.
Take the spotlight
off yourself and shine
it on others.

– Tavis Smiley

Forgive your parents, forgive your siblings, forgive your mate, forgive your friends, and forgive your enemies. Above all, forgive yourself.

– Tavis Smiley

Part of working on yourself is learning how to support another person in being the best they can be. Partners are meant to help each other access the highest parts within themselves.

– Marianne Williamson

Achievement doesn't come from what you *do*, but from who you *are*. Your worldly power results from your personal power. Your career is an extension of your personality.

– Marianne Williamson

Begin today with the image of the *end* of your life as your frame of reference by which everything else is examined. Each day will then contribute to the vision you have of your life as a whole.

– Stephen R. Covey

The next time you have a disagreement or confrontation with someone, attempt to understand that person's concerns. Address these issues in a creative and mutually beneficial way.

– Stephen R. Covey

What's the big hurry? You're not ever going to get it done, so what are you racing toward? Every single activity that you're involved in is for one purpose only, and that is to give you a moment of joy.
Lighten up.
Laugh more.
Appreciate more.
All is well.

– Abraham-Hicks

Reach for the feeling of well-being first, and everything else will fall into place. Be selfish enough to follow your bliss, and you will tap in to the natural, pure, positive essence of you.

– Abraham-Hicks

It's important to only think about what you desire, not what you fear.

– Doreen Virtue, Ph.D.

Know
that you deserve
to receive good
in all ways.

– Doreen Virtue, Ph.D.

By doing your best, the habits of misusing your word, taking things personally, and making assumptions will become weaker and less frequent with time.

— DON Miguel Ruiz

Love yourself, love your neighbor, love your enemies, but begin with self-love. You cannot love others until you love yourself. You cannot share what you do not have. If you do not love yourself, you cannot love anyone else either.

— DON Miguel Ruiz

Celebrate all that is good and blessed about your life, realizing that gratitude is a powerful remedy. Appreciating your blessings increases the vitality of your life force.

– Caroline Myss and Peter Occhiogrosso

Even the slightest change in your diet can generate a new body and a fresh mind. Avoid eating anything today that creates conflict in you. Observe how instantly your body manifests a grateful feeling.

– Caroline Myss
and Peter Occhiogrosso

Even though there may be one truth, be aware that many approaches lead to this truth.

– Brian L. Weiss, M.D.

You will not die when your body dies. A part of you goes on. You will be reunited with your loved ones because they're also immortal.

– Brian L. Weiss, M.D.

Understand the power of partnership—whenever you work with one or more synergistically, your power becomes exponentially greater than it could ever be individually.

– Christiane Northrup, M.D.

Your intellect must always serve the wisdom of your heart. Allow them to be partners. The mind is a great servant but a tyrannical ruler.

– Christiane Northrup, M.D.

Take a
30-second vacation.
Go within and focus
on the positive,
thereby creating
an attitude built
of strength,
courage, and
infinite possibilities.

– Keith D. Harrell

The difference between ordinary and extraordinary is that little "extra." Today, demand more of yourself than you or anyone else can expect.

– Keith D. Harrell

Set boundaries. Protect your precious time and energy.

– Cheryl Richardson

Take a risk. You have the power within to move mountains.

– Cheryl Richardson

God is watching out for you. If you ask Him, He'll tell you where not to go. Your part is to pray for protection from evil, to thank Him for His care, and to obey.

– Dr. Bruce Wilkinson

If sin is the problem, repent and turn around. You'll never regret it.

– Dr. Bruce Wilkinson

Are you willing to stop "people-pleasing" today? The best way to honor yourself is to mean *no* when you say no, and *yes* only when you really want to say yes!

– Iyanla Vanzant

Until today, you may not have understood that harboring feelings creates tension in a relationship, and that what you feel is an important step toward healing yourself and another. *Just for today,* lovingly express your feelings in a way that honors yourself and others.

– Iyanla Vanzant

We fear facing life alone. For fear of not fitting in, we take the drugs. For fear of standing out, we wear the clothes. For fear of appearing small, we go into debt and buy the house. When you know that God loves you, you won't be desperate for the love of others.

– Max Lucado

So what if someone was born thinner or stronger or lighter or darker than you? Why count diplomas or compare résumés? What does it matter if they have a place at the head table? You have a place at *God's* table.

– Max Lucado

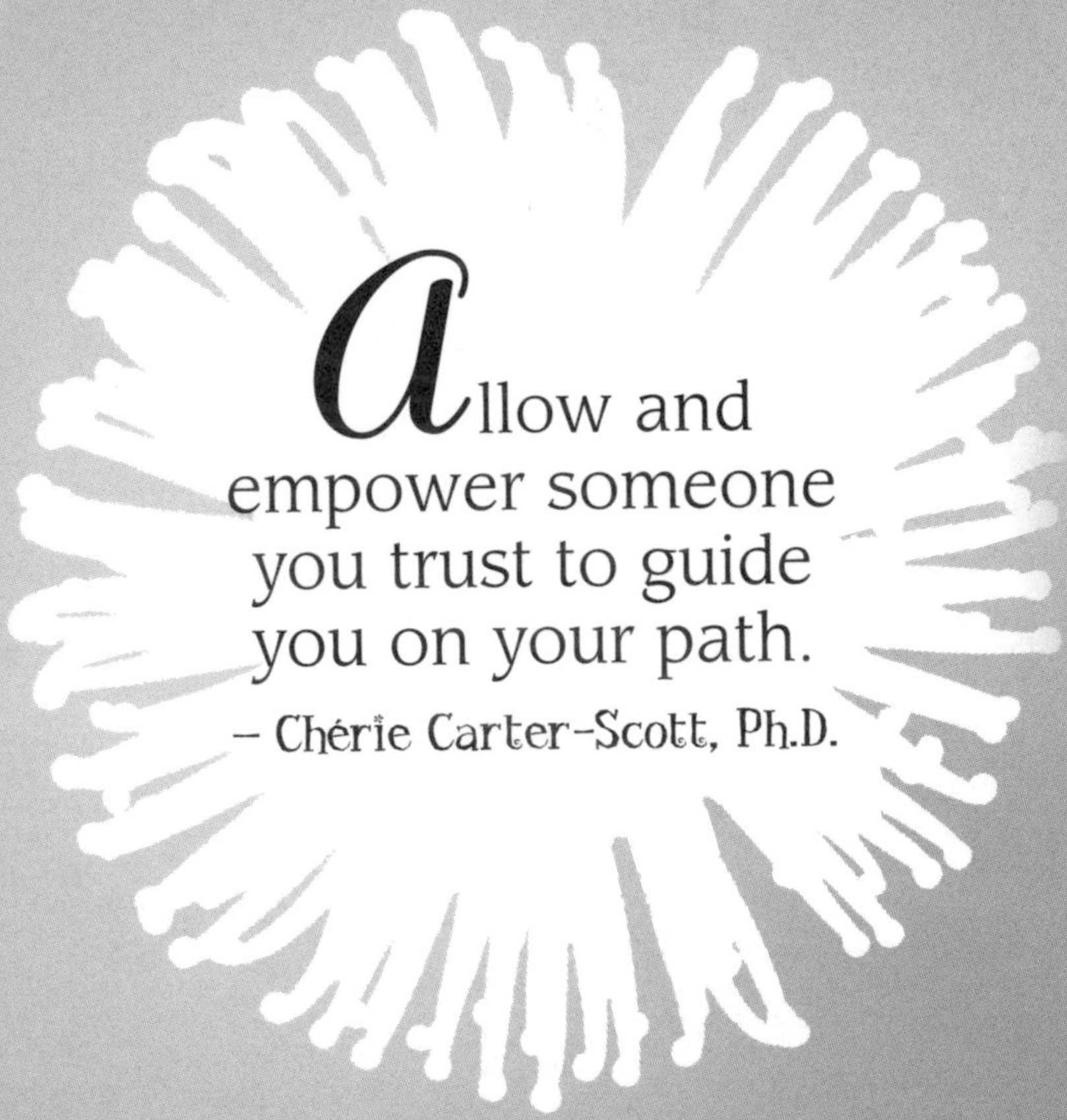

Allow and empower someone you trust to guide you on your path.

– Chérie Carter-Scott, Ph.D.

Embrace another in their totality, and support them in all their dreams.

– Chérie Carter-Scott, Ph.D.

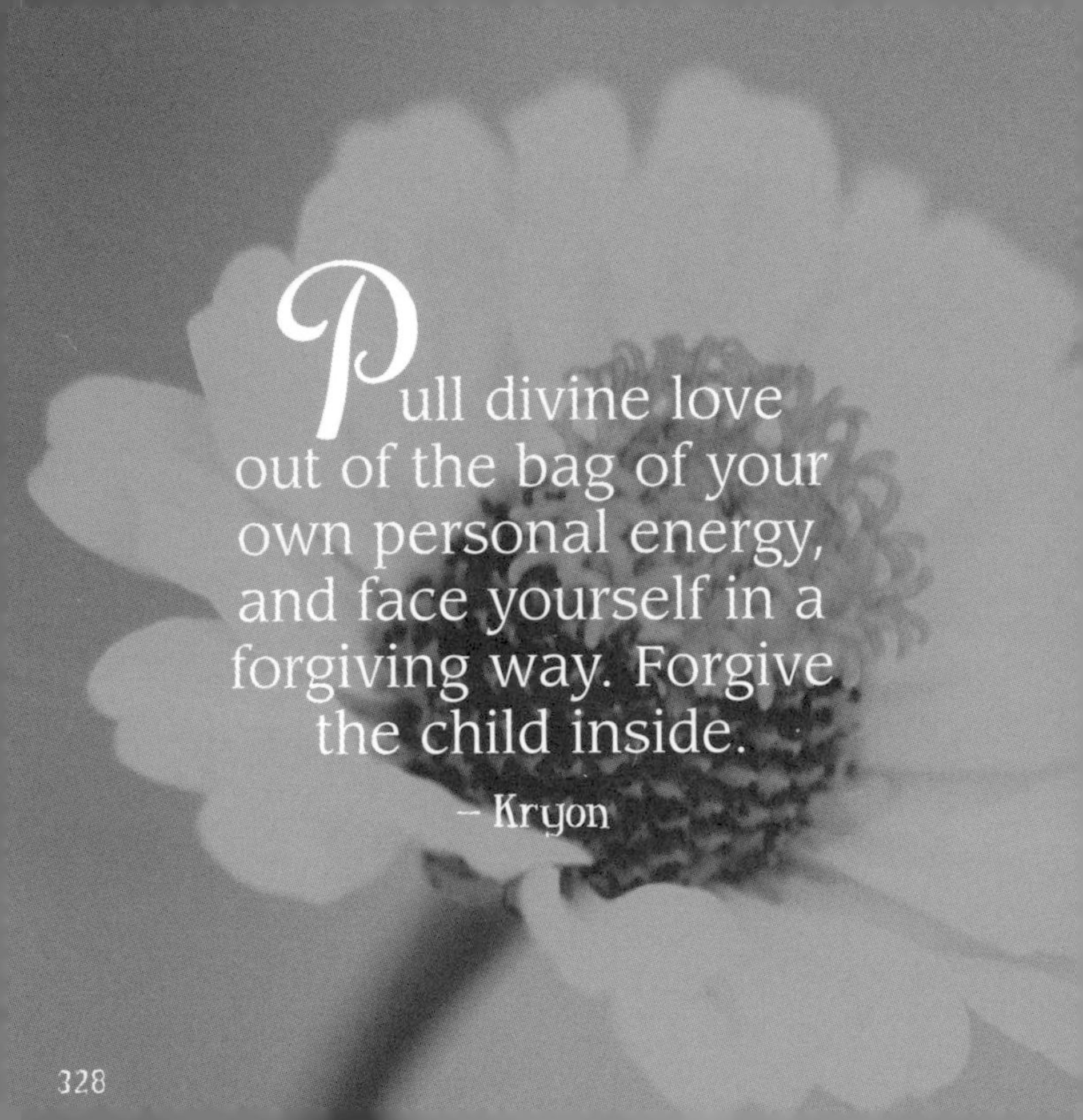

Pull divine love out of the bag of your own personal energy, and face yourself in a forgiving way. Forgive the child inside.

– Kryon

When you call upon the love of God and exercise pure intent, there will be miracles.

– Kryon

You've made some bad choices, you've made some good choices, and you've made some so-so choices. Most important, they're yours—all of them.

– Anne Wilson Schaef

What a delight to know that you have within you all you need in order to know and experience your spirituality. You *are* your spirituality. You need only step out of the way.

– Anne Wilson Schaef

Men,
take her side
when she's upset
with someone.
Women, tell him,
"It's not your fault."

– John Gray

She values
love,
communication,
beauty,
and relationships.
He values
appreciation,
admiration,
recognition,
and trust.

– John Gray

Use a kindergarten classroom as a model for organizing any space. Identify three to five main functions for your room, and divide the space into corresponding activity zones.

– Julie Morgenstern

Some memorabilia is a wonderful treat—too much is overwhelming. Turn a beautiful trunk into a treasure box, and keep only what will fit inside.

– Julie Morgenstern

Rejoice
in your sexuality.
It's normal and
natural for you.
Appreciate the
pleasure your body
gives you.
It's safe for you
to enjoy your body.

– Louise L. Hay

Money
is energy and an
exchange of services.
How much you have
depends on what you
believe you deserve.
– Louise L. Hay

Being relaxed, at peace with yourself, confident, emotionally neutral, loose, and free-floating—these are the keys to successful performance in almost everything you do.

– Dr. Wayne W. Dyer

The choice
is up to you.
It can either be
"Good morning, God!"
or "Good God—
morning!"

– Dr. Wayne W. Dyer

I believe that you must forgive whenever possible, but sometimes there are certain things or people you cannot forgive, no matter how hard you try. This is when you must give it to God, for God is greater than you are and can take care of whatever you can't.

– Sylvia Browne

Rumors will always abound, and the more you do in life, the more you'll be a target. If you're doing what you feel God wants, then rumors won't hurt you. But also be careful that *you* are not the one starting or spreading rumors.

– Sylvia Browne

When you allow yourself to be unpredictable, you step from the known into the unknown, where anything is possible.

– Deepak Chopra, M.D.

Being in love can make you feel so powerful— it can make you feel as if all kinds of wild and wonderful things are possible.

– Deepak Chopra, M.D.

Ask yourself, "What am I telling myself I can't do with respect to money?" Once you've faced your fears and have achieved one of those things you thought you couldn't do, then you'll have to wonder what *else* you're not doing in your life that you obviously *can* accomplish.

– Suze Orman

What happens to your money directly affects the quality of your life—not your stockbroker's life or your banker's life, but *your* life.

– Suze Orman

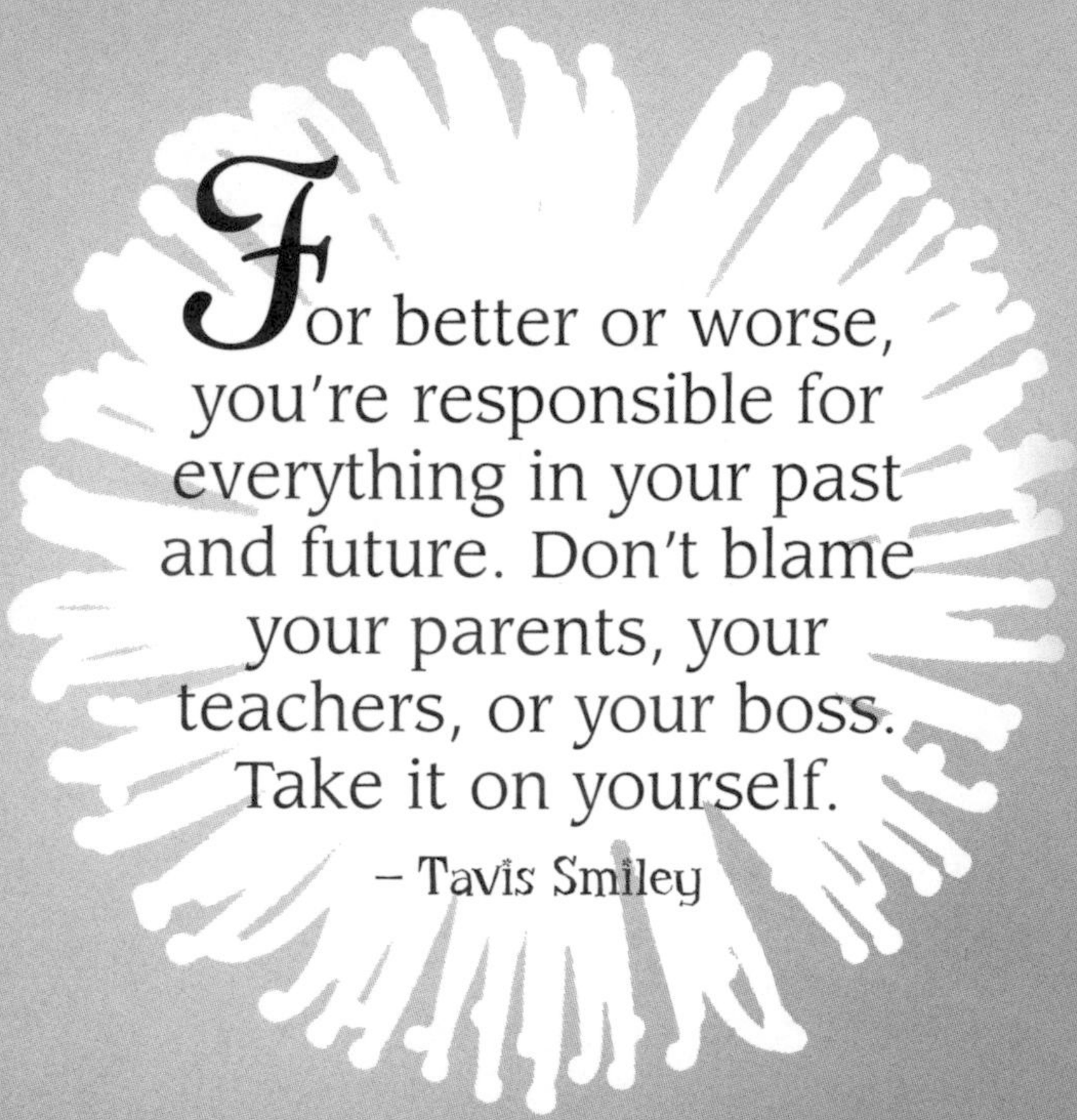

For better or worse, you're responsible for everything in your past and future. Don't blame your parents, your teachers, or your boss. Take it on yourself.

– Tavis Smiley

Surround yourself with people of equal or greater ability, aptitude, and experience. Tap in to new talent, and experience greater growth. Not only will *you* benefit, but those around you will also prosper.

– Tavis Smiley

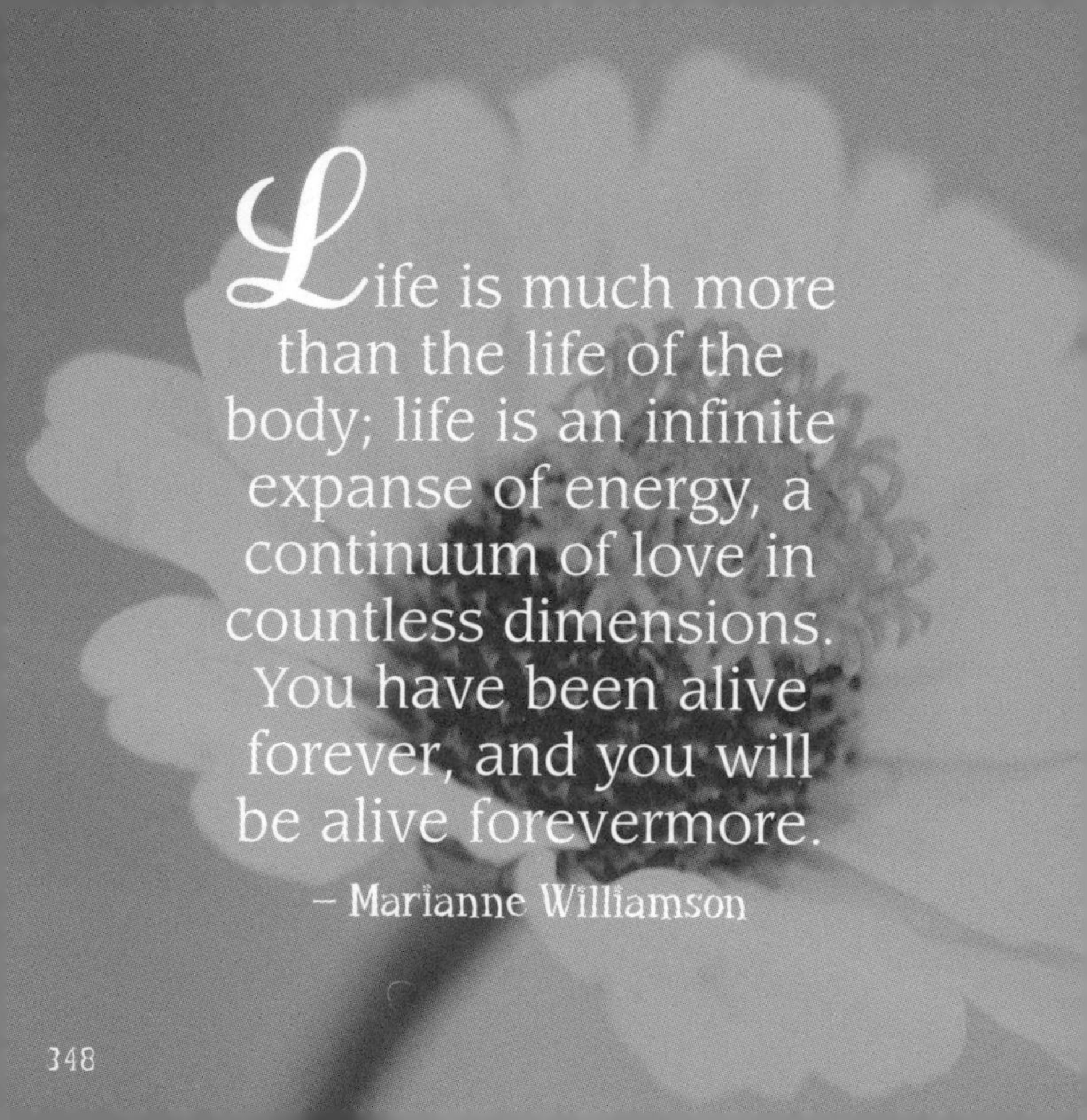

Life is much more than the life of the body; life is an infinite expanse of energy, a continuum of love in countless dimensions. You have been alive forever, and you will be alive forevermore.

– Marianne Williamson

Your greatest opportunity to positively affect another person's life is to accept God's love into your own. By *being* the light, you *shine* the light—on everyone and everything.

– Marianne Williamson

Look at the weaknesses of others with compassion, not accusation. It's not what they're doing or should be doing that's the issue. The issue is your own chosen response to the situation and what *you* should be doing.

– Stephen R. Covey

Valuing the differences between people is the essence of synergy. Truly effective people have the humility to recognize their own perceptual limitations and appreciate the resources available through interactions with others.

– Stephen R. Covey

No effective guidance will ever be achieved by seeking the approval of others, for they all desire different things of you. Constant, pure guidance from Source comes forth from within you. It is always there.

– Abraham-Hicks

The essence of all that you appreciate is constantly flowing into, and creating, your reality. As you appreciate, your state of appreciation opens more channels that allow you more for which to feel appreciation.

– Abraham-Hicks

Work on becoming more authentic and sincere. Release all pretensions and the need for appearances.

– Leon Nacson

Spontaneously engage in acts of benevolence and generosity.

– Leon Nacson

Your heart can create any amount of love, not just for yourself, but for the whole world. Open your heart, open your magical kitchen, and refuse to walk around the world begging for love. In your heart is all the love you need.

— DON Miguel Ruiz

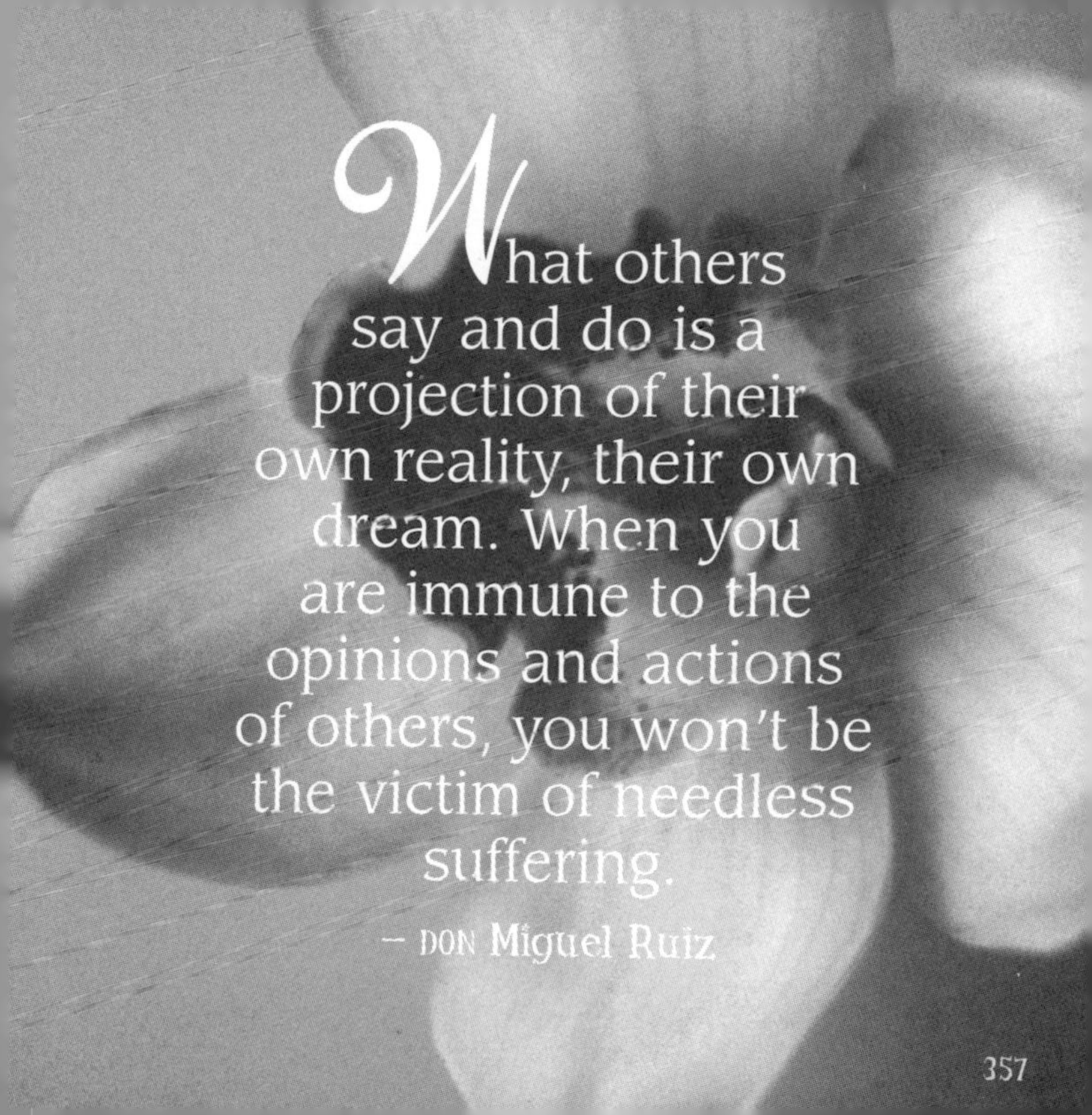

What others say and do is a projection of their own reality, their own dream. When you are immune to the opinions and actions of others, you won't be the victim of needless suffering.

— DON Miguel Ruiz

For this day, acknowledge the restoring power of hope. Direct that power to bless all that needs healing in your life, including your negative attitudes and disappointments.

– Caroline Myss
and Peter Occhiogrosso

Illness can be a teacher, companion, or challenge—but not a punishment. Still, sometimes its message isn't clear. Ignore the illness. Look for stimulation in the knowledge that you can heal in an instant.

– Caroline Myss
and Peter Occhiogrosso

You may find that your mind is usually filled with unimportant thoughts. Focus on your breath or your steps. Every breath is holy; every step is sacred.

– Brian L. Weiss, M.D.

You won't miraculously become happy if someone else changes, or if the outside world changes, but only if *you* change.

– Brian L. Weiss, M.D.

Be willing to admit that you're wrong or have made a mistake. It's the only way to learn.

– Christiane Northrup, M.D.

Give thanks for the great artists, musicians, scientists, and so on, whose work and vision uplift us all. Whether expressing yourself or appreciating the expression of others, you are part of this magnificent circle of self-expression.

– Christiane Northrup, M.D.

Begin to see
the invisible . . .
so that you can do
the impossible.
Your positive attitude
enables you to see
beneath the surface
so that you can
accomplish
anything you want.

– Keith D. Harrell

Tap in to the unlimited mind of creation and draw from it the right thoughts, plans, and actions that will lead you to your ultimate success.

– Keith D. Harrell

Play
with a child.
Children are your
greatest teachers.

– Cheryl Richardson

Ask
for help.
Receiving is an
act of generosity.

– Cheryl Richardson

God has entirely different ways of enlarging your influence and impact. He will arrange circumstances and opportunities that are more strategic for you. It will be as if God has become your Master Scheduler.

– Dr. Bruce Wilkinson

God doesn't expect you to seek out or enjoy His correction. If you're being disciplined, He wants you to get out of it even more than you want to.

– Dr. Bruce Wilkinson

Where in your life are you avoiding a choice? Are you willing to make self-honoring choices today? If you don't make clear and conscious choices, you'll be stuck with whatever shows up.

– Iyanla Vanzant

Until today, you may have been waiting for someone to tell you something or give you something that would make you feel okay. *Just for today,* give *yourself* permission to be okay with yourself. Accept that who you are and where you are—is just right!

– Iyanla Vanzant

Your heart is not large enough to contain the blessings that God wants to give. He pours and pours until they literally flow over the edge and down on the table. The last thing you need to worry about is not having enough.

– Max Lucado

Don't start tackling tomorrow's problems until tomorrow. You don't have tomorrow's strength yet. You simply have enough for today. We don't need to know what will happen tomorrow.

– Max Lucado

Formulate markers that acknowledge your progress and show you where energy or effort is needed.

– Chérie Carter-Scott, Ph.D.

Live in alignment with your values, vision, abilities, and potential.

– Cherie Carter-Scott, Ph.D.

Assemble together and provide positive thought energy for the planet and the Human race. In the new energy, you can create a great deal more than the sum of the whole.

– Kryon

The earth and the Human in lesson are an inseparable partnership. You cannot be balanced unless you understand your root partnership with the planet—through your connection with the heart of the earth.

– Kryon

When you speak the truth as best you can, you're adding to the healing energy of the universe.

– Anne Wilson Schaef

You can never repay all you've been given by the Creator. Accept the gifts. Live and share them.

– Anne Wilson Schaef

Men, think out your thoughts before you express anger toward her. Women, use soft language when you express your anger toward him.

– John Gray

Feminine awareness is expansive—taking in the whole picture to discover the parts within. Masculine awareness tends to be sequential—building a complete picture from each part.

– John Gray

If you put something in its proper home, you'll feel so good when you go to look for it—and there it is!

– Julie Morgenstern

Chaos can provide a sense of comfort, safety, distraction, and protection in your life. Identify the hidden stakes you may have in clutter.

– Julie Morgenstern

Say "Out"
to every negative
thought that comes
into your mind.
No person, place,
or thing has any power
over you, for you are
the only thinker in
your mind. You create
your own reality and
everyone in it.

– Louise L. Hay

You
are the only person
who has control over
your eating habits.
You can always resist
something if
you choose to.

– Louise L. Hay

Treasure your physical being as a vehicle that houses your soul. Once you have the inner way, the outer way will follow.

– Dr. Wayne W. Dyer

You get world peace through inner peace. If you've got a world of people who have inner peace, then you have a peaceful world.

– Dr. Wayne W. Dyer

Everyone has the ability to *be* psychic (but not necessarily *be a* psychic). If you do decide to follow this path, have the courage to go with your first impression, and don't be afraid you'll be wrong. Get your ego out of the way, and get in touch with your own intuition.

– Sylvia Browne

If you feel bored, do *something*, for there is always something to do, see, or explore in this world. Keep in mind that boredom can also cause depression, so get out there and live!

– Sylvia Browne

Meditation allows you to go beyond the mind and get in touch with Spirit. Get to know the "unified field" intimately, where true success in all fields of endeavor is possible—instantly.

– Deepak Chopra, M.D.

What you dismiss as an ordinary coincidence may be an opening to an extraordinary adventure.

– Deepak Chopra, M.D.

When you understand that your *self*-worth is not determined by your *net* worth, then you'll have financial freedom.

– Suze Orman

Giving money
month-in, month-out,
is a way of saying
thank you to the world,
and also a way
of saying *please*.
A pure, charitable
gift will always
be returned—
many times over.

– Suze Orman

What you say and how you say it creates a lasting impression on all who hear you. Expand your vocabulary, and you will increase your impact.

– Tavis Smiley

Take your focus off of how others see you. Cease being obsessed with the need to impress your friends and your foes. Keep your concern on the vision you see in the mirror. Don't allow the approval of others to obstruct your view of *you*.

– Tavis Smiley

Eating nutritious food supports you in living lightly and energetically within the body. In taking care of the body, you take better care of the spirit.

– Marianne Williamson

Peace is much more than the absence of war and violence; it is a condition unto itself. The goal at this point must be the *creation* of peace. Without love, there is no peace. Where love is absent, war of some kind is inevitable.

– Marianne Williamson

Believe in other people even if they don't believe in themselves. Listen to them and empathize with them. Help them affirm their positive traits. Doing so increases the opportunities for interaction with other proactive people.

– Stephen R. Covey

To keep progressing, you must learn, commit, and do—learn, commit, and do—and learn, commit, and do all over again.

– Stephen R. Covey

Say little.
But when you
speak, utter gentle
words that touch
the heart. Be truthful.
Express kindness.
Abstain from vanity.
This is the Way.

– Daniel Levin

Treat everyone and everything with loving compassion. When you see no difference between the sacred and the profane, the saint or the sinner, that is the ultimate wisdom.

– Daniel Levin

Always anticipate the best outcome for yourself and others.

– Leon Nacson

Strive
to achieve your
heart's desires and
to release the desires
that do not serve you.
– Leon Nacson

When you hear an opinion and believe it, you make an agreement and it becomes part of your belief system. The only thing that can break this agreement is to make a new one based on truth. Only the truth has the power to set you free.

— DON Miguel Ruiz

If you have the eyes of love, you see love wherever you go. The trees are made with love. The animals are made with love. Everything is made with love. When you perceive with the eyes of love, you see God everywhere.

— DON Miguel Ruiz

Scale the wall of negativity and self-doubt and refuse to allow any obstacle to separate you from the attainment of your dreams.

– Keith D. Harrell

Today's preparation determines tomorrow's achievement. Live each day preparing for the multitude of opportunities that are to come.

-- Keith D. Harrell

Do something just for fun. Pleasure is one of life's essential nutrients.

– Cheryl Richardson

Own your magnificence. The world needs your brilliance and grace.

– Cheryl Richardson

Do
something new—
or at least different—
every day.
Know that life
is never stuck,
stagnant, or stale,
for each moment is
ever-new and fresh.

– Louise L. Hay

From time to time, ask those you love, "How can I love you more?" Enduring, loving relationships will brighten your life.

– Louise L. Hay

Do
the right thing . . .
especially when
no one is watching.

– Chérie Carter-Scott, Ph.D.

Discover the blessings you already have.

– Chérie Carter-Scott, Ph.D.

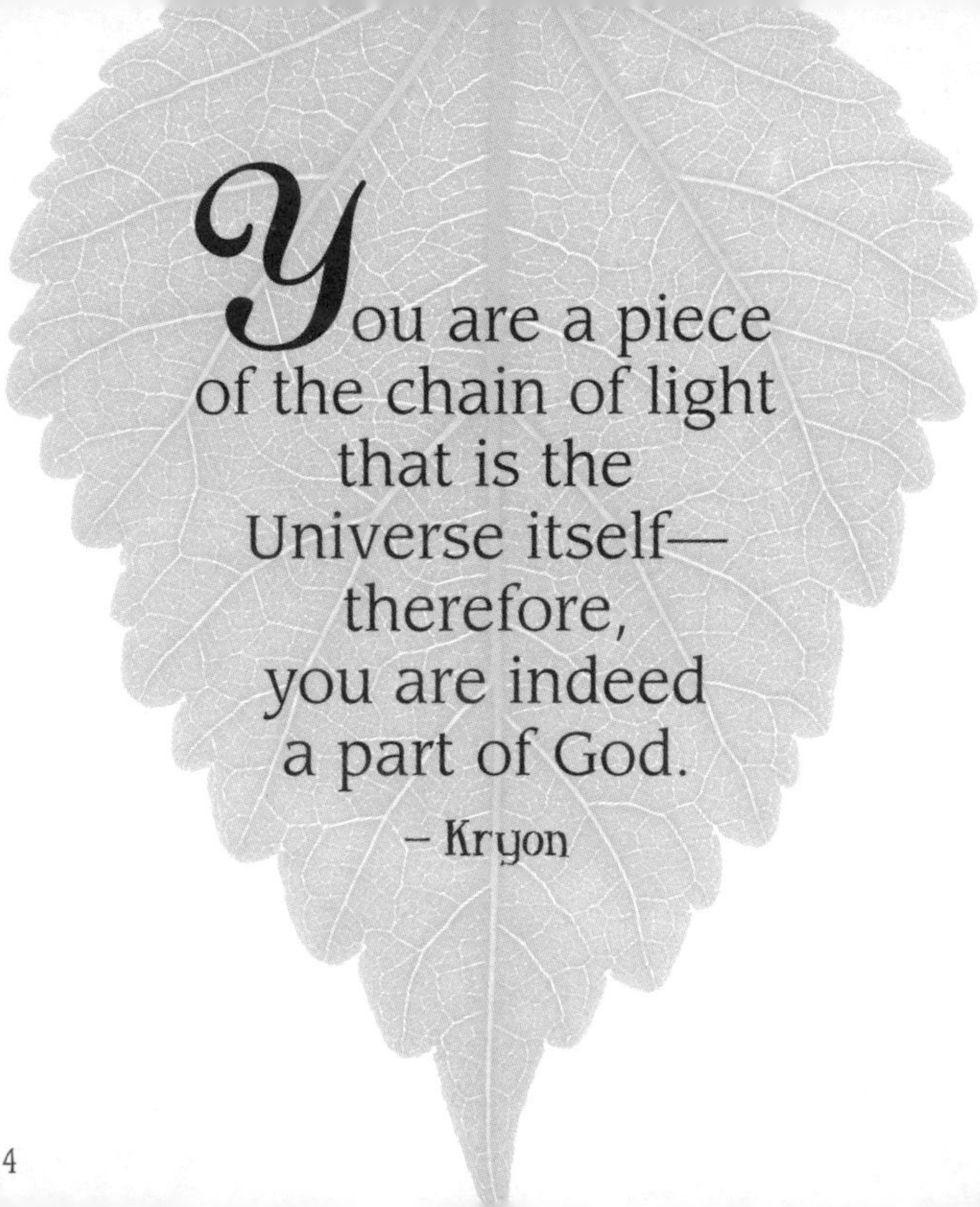

You are a piece of the chain of light that is the Universe itself—therefore, you are indeed a part of God.

– Kryon

Celebrate your life no matter where it takes you—no matter how difficult—and know that it is only a transition.

– Kryon

What wound
have you left unhealed?
Are you willing
to begin healing today?
An unhealed wound
drains you of the
very energy needed
to live beyond
the wound.

– Iyanla Vanzant

Until today, you may have been holding on to things for fear that they would not be replaced in your life. *Just for today,* imagine what your life would be like if you were to receive something *better* than what you're holding on to right now.

– Iyanla Vanzant

From the dawn of time, God has known you and loved you. He's not waiting today for you to get it together. He's waiting for you to come to Him with open, empty hands.

– Dr. Bruce Wilkinson

If your relationship with God is injured, apologize today for your attitudes and thoughts. Tell God you have misunderstood His actions and badly misjudged His character. Tell Him exactly how you have felt and why, and ask Him for His forgiveness.

– Dr. Bruce Wilkinson

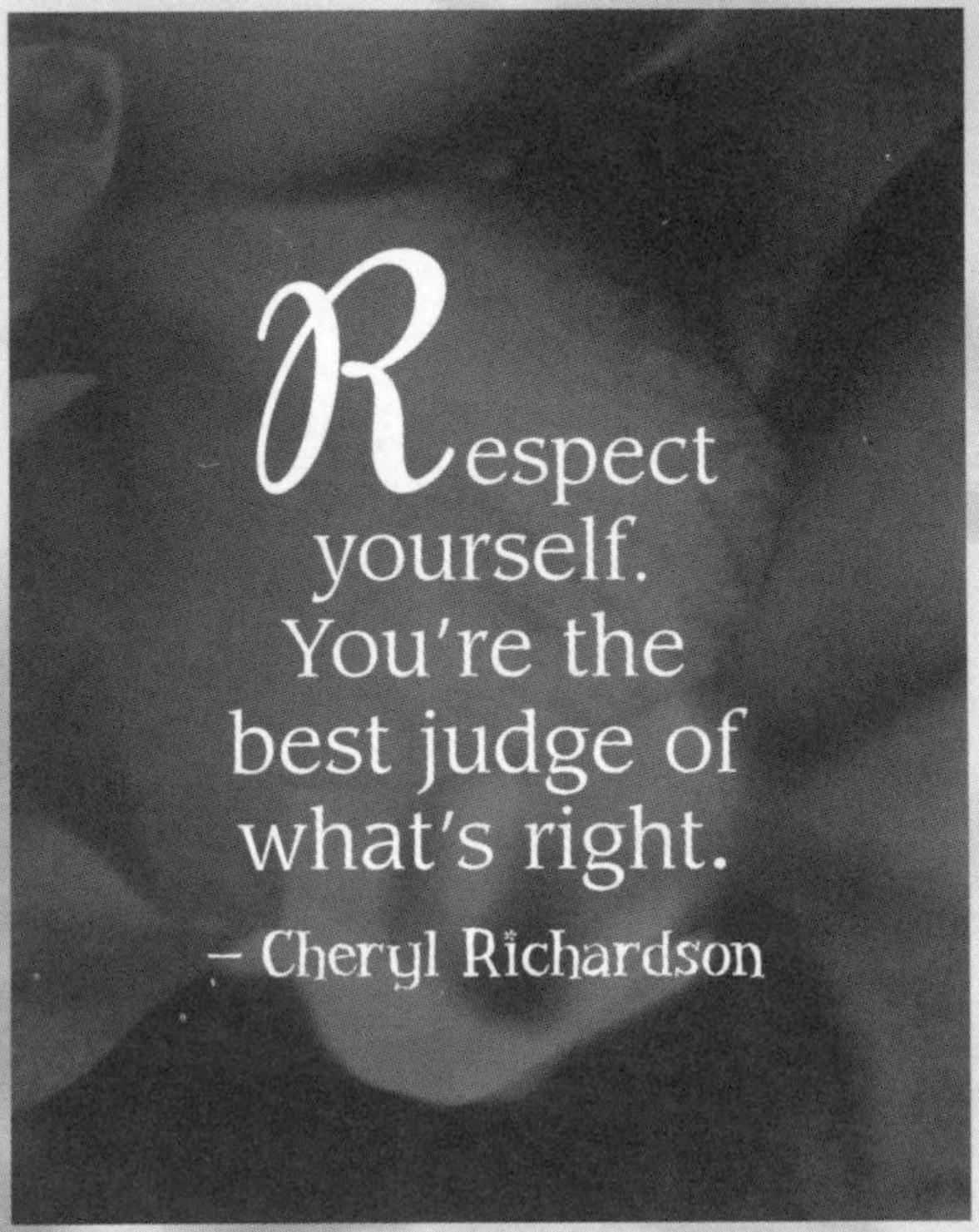
Respect yourself. You're the best judge of what's right.
– Cheryl Richardson

Reconsider a commitment. You have the right to change your mind.

– Cheryl Richardson

Have faith during inevitable conflict. Be willing to hang in there. You never know how something will turn out.

– Christiane Northrup, M.D.

Acknowledge the intellectual and creative contribution of others. Simultaneously appreciate your own.

– Christiane Northrup, M.D.

Words make a powerful impact, and they're not easily forgotten. Wounds inflicted by words of anger or hate can last a very long time.

– Brian L. Weiss, M.D.

Love others fully
and with all your heart,
and do not fear,
do not hold back.
The more you give,
the more will return
to you.

– Brian L. Weiss, M.D.

How do you define "taking care of yourself"? Create a new self-care practice today. Observe your comfort level when it comes to being good to yourself. Discomfort is a wise teacher.

– Caroline Myss
and Peter Occhiogrosso

Practice
the healing power of
a compassionate mind.
Open your heart to
other people without
judgment, and radiate
the message of delight
at having them
in your life.

– Caroline Myss
and Peter Occhiogrosso

Your unique creative talents and abilities are flowing through you and are being expressed in deeply satisfying ways. Your creativity is always in demand.

– Louise L. Hay

Everything in your life—every experience, every relationship—is a mirror of the mental pattern that's going on inside of you.

– Louise L. Hay

You aren't facing death alone; God is with you. You may be facing unemployment, but you aren't facing unemployment alone; God is with you. You may be facing marital struggles, but you aren't facing them alone; God is with you. You may be facing debt, but you aren't facing debt alone; God is with you. You are not alone.

– Max Lucado

Loneliness could be one of God's finest gifts. If a season of solitude is God's way to teach you to hear His song, don't you think it's worth it?

– Max Lucado

Trust is the essence of Win-Win relationships. Because you trust others and they trust you, you can be open; you can put your cards on the table. Even though you may see things differently, you're committed to understanding each other's viewpoints.

– Stephen R. Covey

Taking the initiative doesn't mean being pushy, obnoxious, or aggressive. It means creating an atmosphere where others can seize opportunities and solve problems in an increasingly reliant way.

-- Stephen R. Covey

Illness is a sign of separation from God, and your healing lies in returning to Him. The return to God is merely the return to love.

– Marianne Williamson

Your primary work in life is to love and forgive. Your secondary work is your worldly employment. The meaning of work, whatever its form, is that it be used to heal the world.

– Marianne Williamson

Pick up the pace of your life. Add a new activity, make a new acquaintance, read a new book, or take a new course. Move outside your everyday mundane existence. Add a new beat and expand your boundaries.

– Tavis Smiley

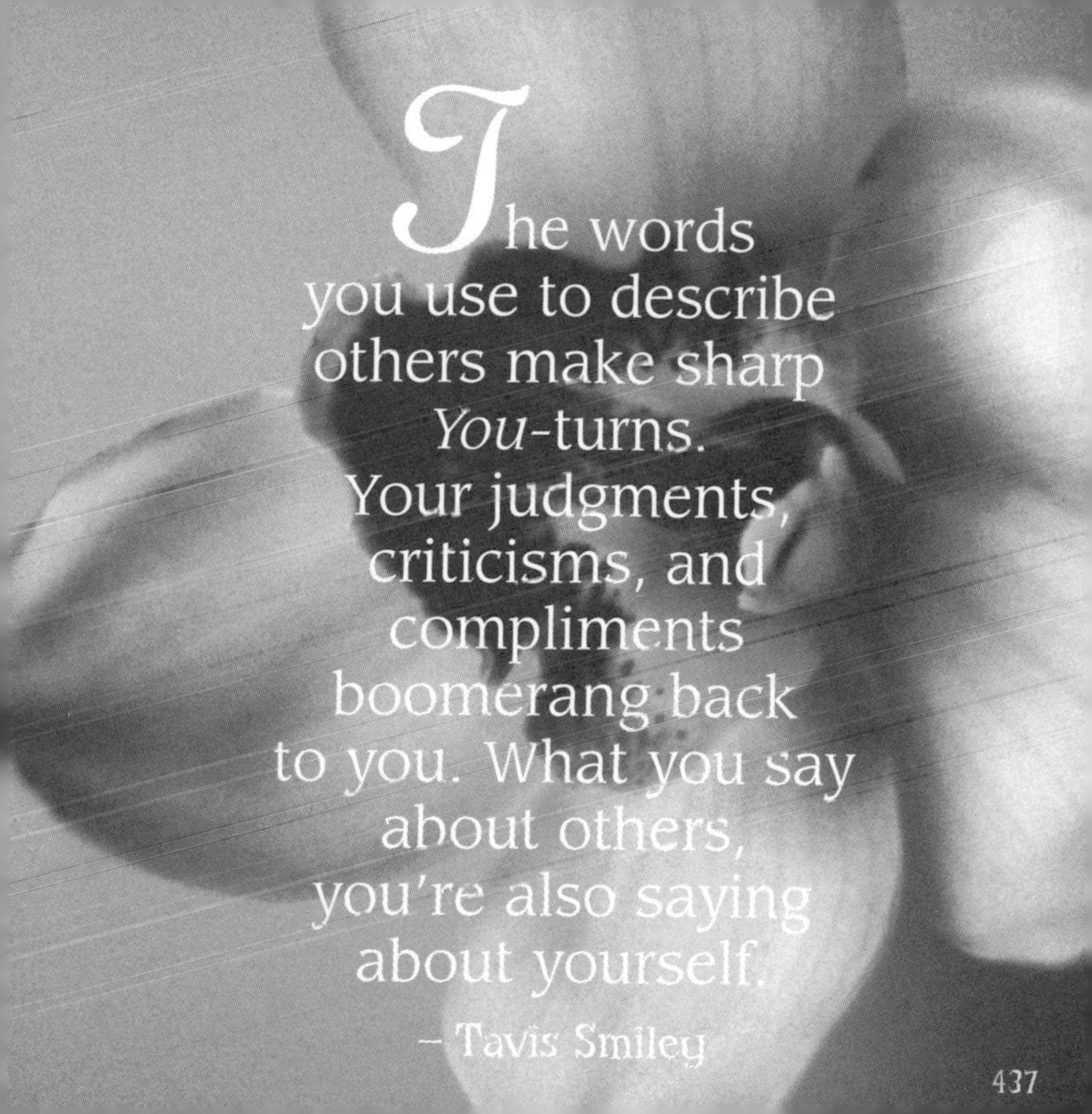

The words you use to describe others make sharp *You*-turns. Your judgments, criticisms, and compliments boomerang back to you. What you say about others, you're also saying about yourself.

– Tavis Smiley

When it comes to every financial decision you'll make for the rest of your life, you'll choose correctly if you go with your first instinctual response. That answer will always be the right one for you, the one that will empower you to make money for yourself.

– Suze Orman

If you want
to change your
financial ways,
just change.
Don't stop
to analyze,
or to ask
why or how.
Just change.

– Suze Orman

How you treat people—whether it be an old friend or a teller at the bank—is indicative of how you can expect people to treat you.

– Deepak Chopra, M.D.

When you recognize and acknowledge your personal power, you no longer need to feel superior or inferior to anyone else.

– Deepak Chopra, M.D.

Your dreams can be a "vent" for all the negativity you've absorbed in your waking hours. Before you go to sleep, just ask God what you would specifically like to accomplish in your dreams, and you'll be amazed at the results.

– Sylvia Browne

God has a great race for you to run. Under His care, you'll go where you've never been and serve in ways you've never dreamed. But you have to release your burdens.

– Max Lucado

Start small.
If you've lived in
chaos your entire life,
create one oasis of
order for now—
no matter how small—
and maintain it for
one month before
moving on.

– Julie Morgenstern

Why organize?
When we're organized,
our homes, offices,
and schedules reflect
and encourage
who we are,
what we want, and
where we're going.

– Julie Morgenstern

Her biggest struggle is maintaining her sense of self while expanding to serve the needs of others. *His* biggest struggle is overcoming the tendency to be self-centered.

– John Gray

Women need to receive caring, understanding, and reassurance. Men need to receive trust, acceptance, and appreciation.

– John Gray

How can you eliminate three things from your lifelong "to-do" list? Are you willing to shorten the list today? Release yourself from the obligation to do things that no longer hold any meaning for you!

– Iyanla Vanzant

There are many truths, but the one that is universal, constant, and unchanging is: *God is omnipotent and perfect.* Everything else is just frosting on the cake!

– Sylvia Browne

Remember that life is very simple. You create your experiences by your thinking and feeling patterns.

– Louise L. Hay

In this new age of enlightenment, you can learn to go within to find your own savior. Know that *you* are the power you're looking for.

– Louise L. Hay

We hope you enjoyed this Hay House book. If you would like to receive a free catalog featuring additional Hay House books and products, or if you would like information about the Hay Foundation, please contact:

Hay House, Inc.
P.O. Box 5100
Carlsbad, CA 92018-5100

(760) 431-7695 or **(800) 654-5126**
(760) 431-6948 (fax) or **(800) 650-5115 (fax)**
www.hayhouse.com®

Published and distributed in Australia by:
Hay House Australia Pty. Ltd. • 18/36 Ralph St. • Alexandria
NSW 2015 • Phone: 612-9669-4299 • Fax: 612-9669-4144
www.hayhouse.com.au

Published and distributed in the United Kingdom by:
Hay House UK, Ltd. • Unit 62, Canalot Studios
222 Kensal Rd., London W10 5BN • Phone: 44-20-8962-1230
Fax: 44-20-8962-1239 • www.hayhouse.co.uk